PRAISE FOR
DIVINELY DIFFERENT

"Jen's ability to walk you through her own story will give you the courage and confidence to live 'divinely different' within your own story. As an author, coach, mother, and encourager, Jen's ability to propel people forward into their purpose is contagious."

Katie Quesada

Speaker, Storyteller, & Coach

"This book will help shift your perspective from different to divine. Oftentimes, the pressure seasons in life are the ones that promote us if we recognize and embrace the opportunity that comes with them. Jen's story teaches us how to do just that."

Sarah Robbins

Author & Coach, SarahRobbins.com

"She did it again! Jen Jones has this ability to not just tell her truth, but somehow tell your truth too. From the introduction and onwards, you will feel as if she's speaking directly to you. This book will give you tools to renew your heart, mind, soul, and spirit. It will also assist you as you take on one of the biggest challenges we all face: how to just be You and embrace your differences wholeheartedly."

Jamil Frazier

Coach, Entrepreneur, & Best Selling Author of *The Twelve Shifts*

"*Divinely Different is a beautiful reminder that we were all born on purpose and for a purpose. Jen's journey of grace and surrender is an inspiration! We can all learn and grow from the way Jen handles life's curveballs. This book is incredibly empowering!*"

Brooke Thomas

Founder & CEO, Live Out Loud

"*This work has been birthed from the trenches of deep surrender. So many are stuck in the cycle of comparison and the never ending climb to fulfillment, but* Divinely Different *shows a better way. Throughout the pages of this book, you will find a path to faith that is grounded in the midst of pain and a hope that is birthed by a God, which directs every step. This book will help you find your way to a life that has been handcrafted just for you.*"

Karrie Garcia

CEO of Freedom Movement
Author, Speaker, & Licensed Trauma Informed Story Coach

"*There is no one like Jen Jones! She lives her life out loud and challenges the status quo. She is one of my dearest and most seriously divine friends who has the unique ability to speak directly with love and compassion. Jen has equipped me* and challenged me as a leader. In Divinely Different, she shares the strategies to create a life awakened to the love and power of Jesus, which is available to all of us. She opens her life up as an example and teaches how to overcome and soar above obstacles to create a life of meaning that makes eternal impact."

Thea Wood

Bestselling Author of *Kick Fear in the Face*

"I've had a front row seat to watch Jen living a life of different in total surrender. No one has embraced a life of hard and chosen to adapt to life's curveballs like Jen has. We now get to benefit from that as she shares firsthand wisdom and tools so we can live our own divinely different life."

Doug Wood

Entrepreneur, Speaker, & Author of "Church Boy to Millionaire"

"Jen's refreshing vulnerability connects to the deep desires in all of us to belong, be loved, and live lives that matter. This book is an invitation to look inward, offer yourself grace, and say 'yes' to enjoying the journey of becoming the best you. I loved it!"

Megan Valentine

Entrepreneur, Speaker, & Author of *No Place Like Known*
Founder of Team Brave

"Jen's book provides her vulnerable, real-time recovery from striving to make a name for herself in the world to accepting and amplifying her divinely different voice. Her candor and openness are generous offerings to the reader."

Tracy Daughtery

Executive Director of the Freedom Challenge

"Jen is a true testament to what it looks like to create a significant life. This book is a world class tool packed with wisdom to help you build a significant legacy filled with purpose."

Brodie Pierson

Top Rated Podcaster & Brand Strategist

"Jen hit the nail on the head with her focus, the world needs this message & this book! Beautifully written!"

Christina Smallwood

Speaker & Influencer

"In this book, Jen speaks straight to the heart of every believer who's thought, 'It wasn't supposed to be like this.' By sharing her own story with vulnerability and honesty, she gently coaches us to let go of what we thought things were supposed to look like and lean into what God's doing in the midst of our crazy, messy, and beautiful lives."

Havilah Cunnington

Founder of Truth to Table

"This is a masterful intertwining of divinity and purpose so readers can live a life of surrender and significance. Bravo, Jen Jones."

Roshanda Pratt

Video Visibility Coach, Producer, Author, Speaker
Founder, The REP Network

"Jen Jones embodies everything she talks about. In this day and age, we need more people who practice what they preach! I am a firm believer in putting yourself around people like that and I believe this book will help us catch what Jen has!"

Elyse Murphy

Author & Speaker

Divinely

DIFFERENT

CREATING A SIGNIFICANT LIFE
WHEN THE WAY IS UNEXPECTED,
UNWANTED, AND UNKNOWN

JEN JONES

DIVINELY DIFFERENT

Cover design by The Good Kids (www.thegoodkids.co).

Published by

STORY ⫿⫿⫿ CHORUS

Learn more at www.StoryChorus.com

FOR THE JONES TRIBE

To Marcus, I would follow you off the cliff over and over again. You are the calm to my crazy. None of these pages would even exist without your faithfulness and commitment leading our family to listen to Jesus and do what He says. I adore you.

To Addie, Tatum, Brody, and Piper, my good and perfect gifts. Without you, I'd have few stories to tell. Thanks for allowing me to put the ones you've lived into print. The deep work of my heart inscribed on these pages are because of you, the ones who matter most.

TABLE OF CONTENTS

INTRODUCTION

The greatest gift God ever gave me was *different*. Different than I expected. Different from what I planned for. Different than what I saw other moms hold.

When my daughter, Addie, was born, her unexpected Down syndrome diagnosis sucked all the air out of the room. Suddenly I had no idea what life would look like, and I was afraid. So many years later, I have come to appreciate that a moment that felt like dying was actually the day my life truly began.

I was being called into *different*, and not for the first time.

I've felt a pull in my heart toward *different* for much of my life. But I've also lived in a world like you do, where loud and powerful forces try to shove me into a box. Be the same as everybody else. Be like her. Behave like them. Be bold but simmer down. Speak up, but also please everyone. Use your voice to coo at whatever the audience is currently listening to. And when they stop approving—because they always do eventually—that is your fault.

It's a confusing message, isn't it? Be uniquely you while also simultaneously fitting in. Find what's working and fit that mold. But also pave your own path.

The day I held Addie for the first time, I heard God's voice shout louder than my internal dialogue. His booming declaration drowned out all the other external noises and voices.

He said, "She is worthy. This is My good work–a Divine work. And it is different. Different than how you might expect My glory to be revealed. Different from what others may value. Different from the beauty you expected to behold. My good work is a different road that many never experience, but it's exactly what I desire for you."

Different is a choice. It does not have to be embraced. *Different* can make you angry because it's not what you would want. *Different* can cause grief to wash over you because of the loss you feel from not getting what you expected. *Different* elicits fear that this unknown will put you in harm's way. But when you embrace difference as a gift from your Creator, it holds so much fulfillment and joy; and it gives you the greatest gifts—those you deeply need—in a way you'd never expect. That's how God operates. That's what God delivers: *divinely different*.

That day I left the hospital changed. In that instant, I embarked on a journey of transformation that would take many years. *Different* taught me to stop comparing. *Different* opened my heart to love big. *Different* helped me see the heart of God. *Different* opened doors.

Different catalyzed authenticity. *Different* enabled me to let go of my "cannots" and focus on my "cans." *Different* was divine, and it was all for my good.

The enemy of my soul lambasted my mind with shame and doubt for way too long. But I have bad news for him. Something divinely different has brought about a revolution of my mind and heart. My faith has always driven my voice. And it will drive my voice now. Through the pages of this book, I pray you will begin to see how the *different* in your life can be the most delightful providence from God. It awakens hope and stirs your soul to consider that some of life's greatest challenges are the starting points of the greatest miracles.

This is the story of a girl who often pined after significance. This is the story of a girl who thought what mattered only really showed up on the big stage. I thought it was about the one who emerged from the crowd and was making the biggest impact in the room.

This is also the story of a girl who wanted to be like Peter—someone Jesus called to step out of the boat. Honestly, sometimes I wanted the part of Jesus, the hero of the story. I wanted to be the one leading the disciples, the one doling out all the hope, the answers, and the ability to rescue even when there is a misstep of faith. In reality, navigating the depths of my own story, I never felt like either. Which left me striving for significance.

That is, until I got super honest. That is, until my story led me to my knees, crying for help. Until I came to a place where I was willing to stop, rest, grieve, and share with people I could trust.

And that's when the story took a turn—the part when I noticed the boat. The boat that carried Peter and the one that Jesus traveled in, too. I have moments when I'm stepping out like Peter and times when I am the hands and feet of Jesus to others. But lots of times, I am the boat. Here's what I mean...

I have found deep significance through divine connection, which looks different than I thought. I'm no longer bound to a hamster wheel spinning through life, never satisfied. I am the boat. I am honored to

> *I have found deep significance through divine connection, which looks different than I thought.*

carry the hearts of people across the rough waters to where they can see the face of their Creator. I am the boat so that when He calls them, they can take their next right step of faith.

I no longer want to be the hero in my own story. Today, I am different. Today, I am the boat.

I wonder what God might be calling you to. It might surprise you how satisfying it is to be divinely different.

"For we are God's handiwork, created in Christ Jesus to do good works, which God prepared in advance for us to do." Eph 2:10

We were each created marvelously different. In fact, you are God's work of art. So be you, in all your intricate detail. It's time to stop believing you would be better if you were me, or her, or them. God has a remarkable plan and powerful promise for you. The time has come to live divinely *different*.

Section 1

IT'S NOT SUPPOSED TO BE THIS WAY

1

IT'S OVER

I was sitting in Chick-Fil-A. It was the same seat, in the same booth, I had sat in every Wednesday for the past seven years. The kids were running amuck in the play structure while I was attempting adult conversation with my girlfriends. I saw his car pull up, and my heart sank. Marcus never interrupted Wednesday at Chick-Fil-A, unless it was serious. Something was wrong, and in my gut, I knew it.

This is it.

Our time is up.

My husband is being pushed out.

For nine years, we had been pastoring at a church in my home city. This job was more than just work—it was our life, our dreams, and our future.

This life was where dreams of ministry for Marcus and me were fulfilled—dreams that had been in our hearts since our early twenties. We had experienced the tremendous joy of helping thousands of people find Jesus and begin a life that follows Him passionately.

It was here, to our beautiful suburban community, that God had sent us for healing after the birth of our first daughter, Addie, who has Down syndrome. It was during this season that my next three babies were born. We bought our first home in a planned community near the church. It was where our kids would grow up with their besties at the neighborhood schools. The Jones Tribe thrived in our little cottage on Flower Pot Lane.

Entwined in this life were also rich relationships. These were our people. We had served faithfully as pastors on this church staff. We'd built lasting friendships and attended neighborhood block parties. These connections had caused me to grow as a person—as a wife and a mom. This community had made me a better leader. This life had included a future of Addie's inclusion. An educational and social process by which she would be educated together and connected with her neurotypical peers. This had been a place of life-giving ministry and abundant opportunity. At thirty-nine years old, it had been a true pinnacle for me. Why would there be an end to all of that?

I silently dismissed myself from the Chick-Fil-A booth, knowing my crew would keep an eye on the kids. And in an instant, in a fast food restaurant parking lot, everything started crashing down around me. My husband looked at me with his head low, and his shoulders shrugged.

"It's done," he said. "There's no longer a job here for me."

No! It can't be. How can they do this? This is our forever home, our community. This is our future, our family. It's the prime of our lives. We're at the top and just getting started. Our kids were born here. God's made a way for Addie in this place. She's going to be the high school homecoming queen...

My inner protests were in vain. We didn't have any say in the matter. In the middle of my life, and at just the beginning of our family, so many dreams in the making were dashed. In what seemed like the pinnacle of our career in ministry, with a clear vision of our future, it all vanished.

I bundled my babies, and we walked out the door of my everyday Wednesday routine. My everyday life. My every day.

And that began the end of life as I thought it would be.

It's worth noting a special irony here: I had just completed the story of my life from the past decade. Precisely at this "Chick-Fil-A" moment, I was on the cusp of the release of my first book. It was a proclamation of God's redeeming power and chronicled the lessons I'd learned from hard things, along with my testimony of what God can do in the moments you least expect.

I called the book, *Thrive: Growing Through Life's Greatest Challenges.* Ironic, right?

Amusingly, I thought the previous decade, with the birth of our firstborn and her Down syndrome diagnosis, had taught me all the lessons on enduring tough stuff. I thought I had earned my stripes; I had done my time managing curve balls and dealing with the unexpected. Ha! As you continue to read, I'm sure you'll agree I was wrong. So, so wrong.

> *And that began the end of life as I thought it would be.*

I thought the release of this book in my community and our influence there would be the turning point to something grand. I considered this writing accomplishment to be the beginning of more advancement in my career.

I had even planned a party.

And now...the life I loved so much was ending.

2

DOWNSIZED

Marcus and I headed to Las Vegas for a couple days of respite amidst the trial we were now unexpectedly thrown into. Vegas is quite clearly the land of excess and bling. It's the city where more is *more* and less isn't really a thing.

At the time, I didn't realize the irony this foreshadowed.

Before we hopped on our flight, I downloaded a long overdue read of the book, *7: An Experimental Mutiny on Excess* by Jen Hatmaker. I'd avoided this book since its release many years earlier. I mean, I thought I was good on "excess." We'd always lived within or below our means, and I couldn't possibly be the rich chick who needed to downsize, right? But I had no idea what was really coming.

The book proved to be a foreshadowing of what was about to be excruciating. Just a few page turns into the introduction and I was already nailed. How am I blind and why? Where have I substituted The American Dream for God's Kingdom? What in my life, and in the lives of most Westerners, is just too stinking much?

Hatmaker described the next seven chapters as exercises in simplicity. Each month would tackle an area that America has freakishly supersized. Upon my return from Vegas, I discovered that my closet was a case in point. I know my strengths and truly know my weaknesses, and I knew that whittling down my suburban walk-in closet would be difficult for me. Hanging on my closet racks were at least three-hundred-and-thirty-six items. Yep! I counted them all because I sensed, at the advent of Marcus' exodus from that church, that something was about to give. I also counted fourteen scarves (because, *duh*, I had a big need for scarves living in San Diego). I tallied fifty-six pairs of shoes. The bags and belts were too unorganized and ridiculously voluminous to count. The drawers were overflowing. But for fun, I counted bathing suits. *Nine.* And to think–I had almost just bought another because it was on sale.

Now, I'm known to be quite a bargain shopper. I usually have a twenty-dollar price point (or so I tell myself...but let's not kid ourselves about those items with spendy designer labels). Even if I had only spent the $20 apiece, the total of just the items I could count added up to more than $8,300. I can't even begin to tell you the expense contained in the ticket price of my accessories. As I inhaled each word of Hatmaker's book, I knew it was coming. My clothing freedom was coming to an end.

I decided that for thirty days I would adorn myself in only seven items. I approached this project like death. A daily part of my routine that oftentimes brought me joy was ending. The little things that made me feel pretty or normal in a season of "momming" littles would have to be denied. A large space in my bedroom that I entered every day and often served as a bit of an adult playground was going to be off-limits. But first, I dressed one last time in my soon-to-be-restricted style. I took my kids to school decked out from head to toe. I adorned myself in three (yes, three) necklaces. I layered t-shirts and a cardigan with another top tied around my waist. It felt like a goodbye. I didn't fully realize what was coming, but that day I began a fast.

A fast can be defined as an intentional reduction, a deliberate abstinence, to summon God's movement in your life. A fast creates margin for God to move. Temporarily changing our routine of comfort jars us off high center. A fast is not necessarily something we offer God, but it assists us in offering ourselves.

Little did I know that this fashion fast was just the beginning. Death to consumption, greed, and the perpetual cycle of want would become a new normal in the next season of my life. Because rapidly following my closet downsize were other, more drastic measures.

In three short months, we would downsize from four bedrooms and four bathrooms in two-thousand square feet of a brand new, custom-curated home in a planned community to three bedrooms and one bath in one-thousand square feet of a worn-out, run-down, slightly renovated 1940's-style home in an urban core neighborhood of our city.

We left the comfort of square footage and gated neighborhoods. We left community pools that mirrored resort-style living. We left affluence and discretionary income, fancy birthday parties, walk-in closets, and high-end SUVs. In one short week, I sold or gave away most of what I had stored up in walk-in closets. I traded it all for a few drawers in an Ikea wardrobe. And even with all the effort to garage-sale or give away, I found myself getting rid of more to live with less as we unpacked boxes from the moving truck. It felt like such a tiny space for our party of six.

I desperately grasped onto my slippery sense of gratitude, but with more and more going out and so little coming in, I questioned how this would work. I was so unsure about how this would be good for my growing family. This new downsized life was just so...*small*.

My youngest daughter was only three at the time. Being the baby and with a little less expectation, we figured she could take one for the girls' team. With only two bedrooms to split between three girls and one boy, we knew one daughter would have to share with Brody. Piper was three and he was five, so it seemed to make the most sense.

"I desperately grasped onto my slippery sense of gratitude, but with more and more going out and so little coming in, I questioned how this would work."

I convinced us all that this was normal. "It's not that big of a deal," I'd say. The city had small houses, and there were other large families. We weren't the first to cram into bedrooms and we most certainly wouldn't be last. I explained "first-world problems" to my children and took pride in their lack of entitlement. But truth be told, every night I pulled out the trundle bed for precious Piper, my mama heart sank a bit. With no money to purchase new, neutral bedding and only enough space for one single bed, we kept my son's previous baseball theme decorations, blankets and comforter. We borrowed an old pull-out from my parents, carefully covered it in a pink sheet, and sweet Piper slept on it each night.

There was just one bathroom for this party of six. This wasn't the most unfamiliar concept. I had spent many nights at my grandparents' house where my mom grew up with her sisters. They only had one bathroom; if they had done it, so could we. I knew it could work, but it did create complications. We had surpassed the phase of "littles" in the bathroom. Family tub time—throwing them all in to wash at once—was not really an option. We were entering the later elementary years with our two older girls. They had begun their preference for showers, and *not* with their brother who was five. This created morning chaos with conflicting messages around modesty. In one breath, it was "Close the door!" In the next it was, "No don't! Dad needs the sink, Mom needs the mirror, and the littlest sister has to go potty."

After school was no different. It was always a rush out of the car to see who would be first in line to the toilet, and the line would stretch through our short hallway for the afterschool bathroom pit stop. Our son decided that waiting was overrated and quickly discovered the bushes in the backyard would suffice. *Ahem*...those plants got more than their fair share of watering.

How did we get here? I kept asking myself, as we tried to shift into this chaotic new normal. *We did so many things right. It's not supposed to be this way. It should not look like this in this season of my adult life.*

Maybe you've been there, asking these same questions. Maybe...

...You walked in for a check-up and the doctor said "It's cancer."

...The baby you dreamed of was born with an unexpected diagnosis that took your breath away.

...Your husband came home later and later from work, and you were blindsided to discover that his tardiness was because of an affair.

...Your job was tense and they were making many changes, but you were loyal and had seniority. That counted for something, right? Except that you were unexpectedly laid off.

...Your best friend betrayed you.

...Your child became an addict.

...You got married, bought the house, began the career, and then it was time to have a baby. You tried for months or more, only to discover that you couldn't conceive. You ran the tests to no avail. You tried and tried and everyone around you was building their family while you were left behind with a dream that seemed broken.

In other words, the rug was literally ripped out from underneath you. You found yourself down on your knees, or head on your pillow, crying out for someone, anyone.

God, do you hear me?

It's not supposed to be this way.

Right?

And sometimes it doesn't end there. So many times, it goes from bad to worse.

3

FROM BAD TO WORSE

We'd been living in our downsized, uncertain conditions for a little while now, and we were doing our best to make the most of it. We had met many of our neighbors and figured out a rhythm that kept us going in our daily routines. It was survival mode, but at least we were surviving.

Well...*mostly.*

On one Saturday before Easter, my husband offered to trim the overgrown front yard of our elderly neighbor—basic lawn mowing and pruning the hedges. It was a small gesture to show our care and clean up our city street's curb appeal. Nothing about it seemed too difficult or too extreme.

After a full day's work and Easter that next morning, Marcus took a shower and headed to bed a little early. I woke up startled by his holler in the middle of the night. "OUCH! I think something just bit me!" I looked over as he stretched out his thumb. I could see what looked like a tiny black pen mark on the very tip. We had no idea what it was, but we both assumed he would be okay. I rolled over and went back to sleep. He tossed and turned as it throbbed most of the night.

Morning came and it was Easter. We headed to church as we did every Sunday. But this day would be anything but routine. By the end of the service, Marcus had red streaks streaming from his wrist up to his elbow. Conveniently, a doctor friend was at the Easter celebration with his family, and I suggested that Marcus show John his arm. As Marcus rolled up his sleeve to reveal what was going on, I hoped John would advise him to just apply a wet paper towel to it. (Wet paper towels work wonders, don't they?) But as this trained physician examined my husband, he calmly looked at Marcus and, with great intent, said, "I think it would be a good idea for you to go to the ER."

Marcus looked at me and hesitated. "It's Easter. We have plans and festivities. Should I just wait until tomorrow? It might be really crowded, and I don't want to miss out on our plans."

But our ordinarily laid-back doctor friend shook his head and said GO. Marcus left for the hospital, and I assumed the duties with the kids. I rushed around, gathering the kids, and getting the side dishes prepared for the full family feast at my brother's house, all the while pretending to not be afraid.

Then, just as my dad said a blessing for the food, my phone rang. It was Marcus. He sounded a little "off" but gently requested my presence.

"They just asked me if I wanted them to use 'heroic measures' to resuscitate me if my heart stops beating. They want me to sign an advanced directive. I think you should be here."

Bad to worse.

I left my kids with the rest of my family, giving assurances that I'd be back soon. But I had extraordinarily little real assurance. By the time I reached the hospital, I was greeted by an operating room nurse. "Mrs. Jones, we're glad you are here. It doesn't look good." I walked into my husband's room as they began to prepare him for surgery. At this point he seemed to be in a bit of delirium, and his body was connected to IV bags full of antibiotics dripping into his veins. The pain was excruciating—his body convulsing. They were drawing blood and running scans to confirm what exactly had entered his body. But no answers.

The doctor soberly questioned me at the side of the bed, as my husband's heart rate pounded in his chest. "If his heart stops beating, do you want us to resuscitate him?"

Are you kidding me? What is happening? We just had Easter service. How did we get to the need for heroic measures? Haven't we had enough, God?

After identifying the pricked finger as the source of all the drama, they surgically scraped out the infection caused by one of those front-yard thorns. Having fought to save his life (and thumb), the medical team were finally able to control the infection that had spread from his hand to attack his vital organs. After five days of recovering in the hospital, Marcus finally came home, along with a home care nurse that continued treatment until his thumb had completed healing.

> *How did we get to the need for heroic measures? Haven't we had enough, God?*

We were both dumbfounded by how this all happened and grateful God had spared his life. But once again we found ourselves in a conflicted space of doing right yet feeling as though it was all going wrong. It was Marcus' do-gooding on the neighbor's hedges that had caused the whole mess.

Meanwhile, our financial situation continued to be stressful. I'd never been one to pine after a lot of money, but wondering if we would have enough to buy groceries was *next-level* anxiety. At one point, I even found myself sitting in the waiting room of our city offices, seeking help for our family of six. As I waited in the government resource building, I stared at the wall with posters for food stamps and family support and wondered for the thousandth time, *How on earth did I end up here? I never planned to leave our white-picket-fence life. How could the church let my husband go? How did we end up like this?*

The city denied me service that day. Turns out we had no income but too many assets. I drove home empty-handed, shaking my head at how incredibly we had been blindsided.

By this time, it was close to Christmas. If groceries were difficult to come by, you can imagine my anxiety over how on earth we would do presents for the kids. We died to any expectation of providing like years past, but the extreme change in our finances left us considering if we should buy *anything.*

That's when I got a message from Marcy.

I didn't know her well, but we had crossed paths a few times at our previous church. I wasn't even sure how she had my number, but she called to say she was in my new neighborhood and asked if she could stop by. A little surprised and unsure what to expect, I met her out front in my driveway.

She didn't even get out of her car. She kindly rolled her window down and passed me a standard, white envelope. "This is for you. Take care of your family. And Merry Christmas." Inside the envelope were five one-hundred-dollar bills. This represented the ability to give gifts to our kids and the rest of our loved ones in a year that felt so desperate.

I was immensely relieved and so, so grateful. God had provided in a way I could not even imagine or make up. He saw me. He saw my kids. And He cared about something as simple as a Christmas present. This empowered me to walk just one more step.

But at the same time, this financial vulnerability was pushing my buttons. I grew up in a traditional middle-class home where my dad and mom worked hard. Overtime shifts, side hustles and layaways ensured that we were never without, so I didn't crave more.

We were also in church every time the doors were open, and I had committed my life to Jesus at an early age. I deeply desired to serve wholeheartedly and make a difference for His Kingdom. Impact has always been more important than nice things.

But here I was, all grown up with four kids of my own to feed, plus hospital bills on top of other basic needs, and I was *uncomfortable*. In one of my sleepless nights of hair-pulling and soul-searching, I discovered a truth in the depth of my heart: Marcus and I didn't get into this "vocational ministry thing" to have a comfortable life...and yet comfort had been given to us anyway somehow. But in an instant, that comfort was taken, and I wrestled with losing it.

The extreme transition left us with four babies to feed and no substantial income. Marcus had been forced to exit his work after giving his absolute best from the best years of his life. He had done really well, only to be repaid with rejection, loneliness, and unemployment. This was NOT supposed to happen to people like us. It's not supposed to be this way!

But it was.

So now what? I asked. *What do we do? How do we serve? More importantly, how do we survive?*

4

I'LL DO ANYTHING *BUT THAT*

I felt myself grasping at straws trying to figure out how this was all going to work out for our good. I told my husband that I was desperate. I was ready to resign all dreams of influence in the American church. I was done. The mission and vision we'd held onto for so many years had abandoned us. Well, FINE.

I'd decided we could both go to work and be traditional instead of missional. We could be the best volunteers any nonprofit has ever seen. I was even willing to go beyond downsizing and move to a third-world country. "I'll take our precious babies to make a life in a village serving people from a hut. But the only thing I will not do is plant a church."

(Famous last words, right?)

You may not know much about church planting. I knew some, though I was convinced I knew it all. For instance, I was aware that most church plants were often started by zealous young pastors in their late twenties or early thirties–the ones with enough naïveté to think planting would be fun and with enough energy to believe that they would succeed and change the world.

This was *not* us. We were in our forties. We had four kids. We felt we had done the hard work and were ready to reap some rewards, not begin again. We were also bruised, deeply wounded, and very tired.

We knew that church plants and start-ups tend to attract unchurched and de-churched people, those who were hurt by the church or decided in the past that it wasn't for them. These folks are often a little grittier than those who follow an established church pastor.

I love people and I love gritty, but I'll admit that I was sad at the idea of walking into a new circle, connecting with strangers, and creating a new community. I thought we had run that race and were headed toward an easier second half. But in fact, we were not. In many ways, the future was looking grim. The percentage of church plant successes was low, and the statistics were not in our favor. Often the failure to thrive was about money—there was just no profit in starting a new church. And the rate of progress for inner-city churches was even less.

Late one Saturday night, hip deep in my fear of the future, I hopped in my car. I left the kids at home with Marcus and decided to drive the streets of my new neighborhood all by myself. Perhaps this sounds a bit silly to you. Even to me, it sounds strange.

As I drove, I reminded myself that I had craved a kind of radical living when I was in my youth. I had *not* envisioned a life with double bob strollers and pretty paved sidewalks in well-constructed suburbs. But after accidentally acquiring one, it felt good. And somehow along the way, it became my kind of normal; I had unintentionally fallen into the trap of desiring something typical instead of different.

In my gut, I could sense that so much of that old, comfortable, "familiar" way of life wasn't working, and my drive was an attempt to dive back into something radical. This new adventure we were on was happening, ready or not.

Behind the steering wheel, I was testing my bravery. I rolled down the windows to immerse myself in the smells and the sounds of my new home in the city. I drove this way for almost an hour. I hit up the freeways and all the alleyways. I drove around the high rises and government buildings that ran the city. These were the skyscrapers that employed the rich and served the poor. I drove through the barrio and slowly passed by low-income housing and shelters that were doing good work for the people of this city. I found grocery stores and privately owned markets. I passed restaurants founded by famous chefs with fancy culinary degrees. I saw mom-and-pop taquerias started by families who had crossed the border now using their culture and skills to serve up homemade tortillas. I watched young people dressed to impress walking toward the hip clubs late on a Friday night, and I passed by families on street corners begging for money to feed their babies.

On some streets, I felt safe—even a sense of excitement. But then I'd turn the corner and be terribly afraid. Dread would overwhelm my heart. When the tension in the darkness became more than I could bear, I rolled up my windows to drown out the noise of my new reality and turned to an old album my husband had written.

I pressed the button on the stereo and a song began to play. Tears began to flow down my face at the drop of the beat, the strum of the guitar and the sound of his voice. The song that played brought back a flood of memories. Marcus had written it a decade previous. He had scribbled out the lyrics on a napkin in a children's hospital cafeteria as our first-born daughter, Addie, lay in a neonatal intensive care unit bed. It was the anthem of our hearts during that time. And now, ten years later, the lyrics still rang true:

"Carry me, cover me. Lord, how I long to be lost in Your love. Breathe your breath of life in me. Teach me and I will know, ask me and I will go now, right now. I'll speak of Your glory, tell of Your wonders, sing of Your greatness to all of the earth. That You are my desire. You are my reward. Everything I hope for. Everything and more. You're my constant dream, my glory and my king. My king. You deserve the worship. You deserve the honor. You deserve the highest place of praise."

This was the cry of my heart—this kind of radical worship and sold-out commitment. And I knew that the difficult, desperate, uncomfortable circumstances thrust on us were drawing me back to that heart cry. It's just that it had all happened so *suddenly*. Within the blink of an eye, my entire world had turned upside down.

Still connected to that heart cry, I returned home. And just weeks after my profound speech and declaration of what I would *not* do, Marcus and I decided we would, in fact, be planting a church...in our city's urban core.

So how was our family of six going to beat the odds and have any form of success? We needed money. And we needed it fast. Little did I know that this need would lead me to say yes to yet another thing I swore I'd never do.

The journey started with me hustling on the weekends. I called up a friend who was a high-end wedding planner. She coordinated for the most affluent families in the most exquisite spaces you could get married in San Diego. "HELP! Is there anything I can do for you in your work?"

That was the day the reality of *bridezilla* came into my life.

Don't get me wrong—many of those clients were very nice. They just had a lot. They grew up with a lot, and they expected a lot. My duties were broad, but primarily my job was to follow the bride and her party of girlfriends around with a tackle box full of safety pins, Tide sticks, lip balm, Scotch tape, hairspray, and deodorant. Although I'd had a wedding of my own, I had no idea all that you might need on your big day. But I'm a good one for fake-it-til-you-make-it and found myself performing tasks I had no business performing because I learned real quick that the answer is never "No" to a bride or her mama on her important day. But no matter the task, the day's worth of work in the Bridezilla industry landed me a measly $250 bucks on Saturdays.

Meanwhile, as I was serving the rich and famous of our city, my husband was interviewing for a job with corporate America. Marcus had both undergraduate and graduate degrees outside of his passion for the church and theology, which brought us relief. Surely he was qualified, and we were hopeful that the hunt for an executive-level business position would work out. But again, to add insult to injury, we were wrong and his corporate pursuit fell flat. With no open doors he found a night job as an adjunct professor teaching worship once a week at San Diego Christian College.

Desperate, I found myself taking a step I would have never expected. An old friend invited me to explore an option that had brought her fulfilling financial success. Like church planting, it was an option I'd always dismissed, thinking, "Thanks but no thanks. I'll do anything but that!"

But of course, things were different now; and I was starting to wonder if nothing was off the table.

This friend had reconnected when she invited me to speak at a women's gathering of some of her friends over my first book (remember—the one I had published when Marcus lost his job). The ladies were lovely and my time with my old friend, Thea, felt like home. She was safe. And because she wasn't part of the last two decades of my life, I shared the financial ruins we were headed into. The more I externally processed, the more she leaned in.

That's when she made me an offer. She shared her work and how it could provide for my family and me. She mentioned mutual friends from our history together that had joined the journey. She said they were experiencing a growing impact while making an income. And then she invited me in. She offered both Marcus and me plane tickets to Tennessee where we could explore if starting a business as a health coach might be a thing for us.

I didn't resist but I did have one condition for accepting her generous gift: no strings attached. I wanted her to know that our rekindled friendship would remain intact even though I was likely to say no to this job opportunity. She agreed and so, unplanned and on a whim, grasping for hope, I flew.

> *I desperately wanted to create a life around what mattered most to me, and these people got that.*

I landed in Nashville and found myself sitting in a large convention room. As I sank into my stadium seat, I listened as very ordinary people began to share one after the other. They spoke of the hope they had discovered and wanted to offer me. The atmosphere resembled my former church experience: a large crowd with loud music, bright lights and powerful stories of transformation. It all had me curious...but also conflicted.

A deep desire to change the world, coupled with my urgent need to provide real-life income for my real-life family, had landed me in a seat at this direct sales national event. I definitely needed work, and the thought of "clocking in" at a conventional job made my skin crawl. This opportunity was different.

I desperately wanted to create a life around what mattered most to me, and these people got that. They passionately communicated with their inspiring stories about their physical changes. They gave hope for a healthy community. And they all defined their profound financial shifts. I had never made a dream board or a task list that had "entrepreneur," "health and wellness," or even "coach" as part of it, and yet I was intrigued.

But I was cautious, too. Everyone else was already a follower. They all belonged here. I was the only skeptic in the room who had not decided yet. I sank deeper into my seat, having a quiet, private conversation with God.

"Lord, you can do anything. You could provide *any* way. I mean, I just published a book. You could blow that thing up! But is this what you want instead? Direct sales? Really? Why would you ask me to work in this way?"

I was a wife, a mom, a pastor, a communicator, and even an author. I never saw this one coming. But could it be something outside of my box that would enable me to provide income and make an impact?

In a short thirty-six hours I went from not even knowing this company—never even hearing its name—to signing up to be a representative. I became both a client of the program and a coach to serve others all on the same day.

It was all shocking, but by this point I was growing increasingly unsurprised at the things I would say yes to. The unexpected, the shift into something different, was becoming more familiar and "on-brand" for the way God had been showing up in our lives.

Do the thing you say you won't. Find the hardest path and follow it. The worst-case scenario, the embarrassing route, what you don't think you want, that's actually *it*. That is the thing. Say "yes!" and do that.

And so, with four kids in tow, I started a business and we launched a church in the same month because well, why not?

Maybe you've been there. Maybe you are there right now. Maybe you have faced a series of undesirable decisions that's left you feeling all alone and trapped. You want to believe that hope is rising, but you look at your circumstances and every option feels *terrible*.

You don't want to work the night shift. You don't want to sell your home. The thought of disrupting your kids' normal seems impossible.

I get it. I felt like God was intentionally asking me to say yes to the exact things I *didn't* want to do. And though I was grateful and willing, I was also grieving and angry. I mean, let's recap what happened in just a few short weeks:

* My husband politely resigned from his position at our church.

* We emptied out our house and packed half our remains into a small U-Haul, destined for our "new," much smaller city house.

* I registered my kids at their new local school, leaving one of San Diego's best-rated school districts to enter the one with the worst reputation.

* We planted a church.

* This was to be done with no income, and we were completely alone.

* To be in partnership with this new endeavor and continue to be home with my kids, I began to build a new direct marketing business in the garage of our one-thousand-square-foot home, completely from scratch.

Oh, and of course the whole "Marcus almost dying from a thorn prick on his thumb" thing. I can honestly say that all of this was a total surprise to me. As each night ended, I feared and anticipated more unexpected (and unwelcome) surprises would appear in the morning. It wasn't supposed to be this way. But this was exactly the way that it was.

"I felt like God was intentionally asking me to say yes to the exact things I didn't want to do."

5

MY GREAT RESIGNATION

Time passed both slowly and quickly during this season,
and before I knew it, the weeks had blurred into years. Despite my
dramatic tendency to believe in extremes, it eventually became clear
to me that no one in our Tribe was going without. There wasn't one
hungry child–not even for a day. And the house we lived in increased
my faith. The very thing I had dreaded–our downsizing and relocation–
became the thing that most impacted and transformed me. Amazing
what God can do with four walls, three bedrooms, a single bathroom,
and a family surrendered.

The church was also growing, and we had hired a full staff. The
house's poorly insulated garage served as church offices and became
proof to me that, if we are faithful with little, God will trust us with
much. We soon outgrew that garage, and our growing staff ultimately
landed a sweet creative loft space in the heart of the city.

Even more, my business was taking off. So much so that we were
able to move into a new house. The new place was only four blocks
away (I can see our old one from my patio as I type). It was a big

house–really big–for our neighborhood. It had four bedrooms, four bathrooms and a yard with a pool for our Tribe.

So there we were, a few years after we'd started, living in a big, beautiful, dream home for my family. We had built a stable church community and a business that was growing. In so many ways, we had risen from the rubble like Job. We had persevered through the pain, and by all appearances, we were excelling. But deep down there was a longing to build something more than stable. We wanted something explosive.

> *We had persevered through the pain, and by all appearances, we were excelling.*

I craved more: to be more known, more seen, more influential. The insatiable desire was driven by "self," and most days, I depended on it too. This reality left me with a constant tension beneath the surface that I often avoided or attempted to dissuade by continuing to pursue achievement. If only I could just be number one.

And then one tiny piece of mail caused things to crash around me again.

The incident in question happened the week before Easter. Now, it's important to know that Easter weekend is like the Super Bowl in the church world. Normally I LOVED this day. I loved the new outfits (pretty frilly dresses with lace for me as a kid in the eighties, Miami-Vice-inspired blazers draped over flashy t-shirts in my teens...), the special musical productions telling the story of Jesus, the full pews on Sunday morning, the family feast afterward. I looked forward to all of it.

Up until now.

Because I was dreading this Easter Sunday.

As pastors, what was supposed to be the day we celebrate the reason we even have our faith became the day that the rest of our year's success or failure was riding on. The pressure to perform overwhelmed me. It seemed that the measurement of Easter's value had more to do with packed houses and IG candids than remembering the sacrifice of our Lord and celebrating His miraculous resurrection.

In an attempt to ensure greater attendance, we felt pressure to lure people in with curated donut bars and electronic giveaways during easter egg hunts. Or just skip the egg hunt and have a helicopter egg drop instead. It was bigger, better, and faster; and the church that could one-up would win. We couldn't compete. We were a sweet church in the barrio, and in this season of our ministry, big just wasn't going to be us. Our budget was small. Our facility had limits. I felt like we were losing.

Dark thoughts, right? This was where my head was when I walked up our driveway to pick up the mail the week before Easter Sunday. Not much was there but one full-color, postcard-size print that caught my eye.

I knew immediately what it was.

There was a new church in town, and they were launching out this weekend. On Easter. The photos were familiar, the language common, and I almost brushed it off until I saw the address.

I couldn't help myself. I closed the mailbox and beelined down my driveaway. Storming through my front door, I landed on my back patio looking over the canyon, peering into the valley below. *There.* Right across the tree-lined gap between residences was the address of the new church plant. This start-up church community would be gathering each Sunday right in my backyard.

"What's the big deal?" you ask. "Isn't it great to have more Christ-followers doing excellent work in the city? Isn't it Biblical? Isn't the harvest full but the workers few?"

Yes! But at this moment, all I felt was threatened. The narrative in my head had me claiming aloud, "This is it. We're toast. It's done."

By this point you might have picked up on the fact that I'm a bit of an external processor. So naturally in my distress, I exercised my option to phone a friend. I called Karrie.

Karrie and I had met quite a few years previously. She had launched a nonprofit at the same time we launched our church. Her work serves as a catalyst for change by creating safe places that foster healing, hope and the courage to love who God created you to be. Karrie and I made an instant connection, and we often felt uniquely understood by each other. Thus, on this day I knew Karrie would get it. And even more so, she wouldn't judge. Deep inside I knew I wasn't thinking clearly. But when the amygdala (the primal fight-or-flight center of the brain) has taken over, it's hard to stop the spinning and see straight.

Bless Karrie, because I panicked during the call. My heart was racing, and I was pacing the deck. I don't remember every word I said, but essentially it went something like, "Karrie, it's over. We're dead. I can't do this anymore...I want to quit."

That's when she interrupted my blubbering and with full authority said, "Jen, you need to pivot."

Just like that? Make a slight turn. But toward what?

I was following the direction I had been commanded to go in; and counting a great cost, I willingly obeyed. *So now I'm just done?* I thought. *I pivot? Who will hold my responsibilities? How will this even work? It's our work. It's our church. It's my life and the only way I know it.*

I mean, a pivot DID sound appealing. I could taste the relief. But could I do that? Could I make a turn and go in a different direction, setting down obligations as though they were no longer mine?

With one simple declaration, Karrie's words had opened a door to the unthinkable. And it set me free. My business was going well. It had

"Could I make a turn and go in a different direction, setting down obligations as though they were no longer mine?"

been growing and I was having fun. I had an energy for it and imagined all I could do and become. In contrast, the work in our ministry caused tension in my marriage, and it felt like everything I touched fell flat. I called this "the cost" and assumed that my faithfulness was being developed even if it wasn't enjoyable.

Well, no more. Right then and there, I made my "Great Resignation." I decided to resign from my role in the church.

There are a couple of definitions of the word *resignation*. One is to give up a position. The other is the acceptance of something undesirable or inevitable. By "resigning" myself to demands and striving, I'd been stuck in this second definition for years. And guess what? It was a victim move, like shrugging your shoulders apathetically and saying, "it is what it is."

On this day, I stepped out of a victim's resignation and stepped into the first definition—to give up a position. Rather than slump over under the burden of "carrying the cost," I decided to stand tall and not shrug. It was a proactive stance to let go of my mindset. Release my strife. Go against my routine and disrupt my pattern. This was an act of surrender.

It was also a major turning point in my life.

6

EMBRACING THE PAIN
OF PIVOTING

By this point in our time together, you've heard me detail some rather severe (and for me, traumatic) changes that unfolded in my family in a shockingly short amount of time. There is a lot more to this story. So many tearful mornings and fretful journal pages and angry prayers to God. But this isn't a memoir. This is a book about living differently—divinely so. So why am I going to great lengths to share all these episodes in my journey? Why publicly document the details of what was a very vulnerable and painful time for me?

Because, these experiences led me into so much incredible freedom. The journey, which we're not finished with, was painful. But it was God's divine and gentle (yes–gentle, though certainly it didn't feel so at the time) process for shining a light onto some deeply ingrained patterns and false beliefs that were powerfully shaping my life, and not for my benefit.

In the pages to come, I want to transparently share my heart with you–the heart that was revealed during this crucible of change. I won't lie–parts of it aren't pretty. But I humbly believe that a lot of it is *relatable*.

My "Great Resignation" was the catalyst that opened my eyes to many of these less-than-lovely parts of my heart. Quitting my role at the church may not seem like a significant event (so what if she quit her job so that she'd have more time for her *other* job?), but it was a seismic shift. Seismic because God used it to begin setting me free from performance, striving, and my fear of insignificance.

I acknowledge that it's tempting for me to gloss over this next part and jump to the end, to the unfolding victory. It's more comfortable, and more common, to share my testimony in a familiar format: Things were going well, they fell apart a bit, and then through prayer and some uncomfortable character-building, God fixed it.

> *But to create a significant life, I needed more than just a resolution to my problems.*
>
> **I needed to change.**

But to create a significant life, I needed more than just a resolution to my problems.

I needed to change.

Change is hard, and many of us avoid it at any cost. I know I've tried. But by avoiding change, we create even bigger problems, such as lost opportunities, broken relationships, or even wasted potential. Craig Groeschel said it best, "To step toward your destiny, you must step away from your security." Ouch and Yikes!

My resignation was going to represent *major* change. I had been in vocational ministry my entire adult life—since I was nineteen. I had never worn a different label or pursued any other path. Even my role in business had been secondary—a means to an end, which was to serve my ministry.

Let's look objectively at this because I suspect some threads connect to your story.

First, a pivot away from ministry and into the marketplace full-time meant a loss of identity for me. For my entire life I'd defined myself based on my ministry role. God was about to show me how limiting this was and how He wanted to reshape my identity in new ways.

Practically speaking, quitting the church almost meant a release of responsibilities. This might sound nice in theory, but remember–I was panicking. I had been white-knuckling everything since that fateful day at Chick-Fil-A; and I felt like I was losing, especially in ministry. Letting go felt like failure. God was about to dig into this fear of failure and prompt me to examine its roots deeply.

And while this pivot brought clarity, it also created questions. I believed that a call to vocational ministry was the highest level of purpose, and giving your whole life in service made you truly worthy. If I switched to focusing solely on health coaching, how could I be in good standing with God and the church? God was about to show me what true calling and purpose looked like, and it was different from what I thought.

In sum, the reality was that life in a new occupation scared me. Would I still matter? Was my work in business something that God would define as worthy? And if I'm brutally honest with you, I was worried about what others would think. Would they still admire my efforts? Or would they consider me a sell-out, settling for something less valuable and vainer?

I can't be the only one to have experienced an intense transition like this–where it feels like you're letting go of pieces of yourself. Often those pieces aren't even enjoyable to you–but they're valuable because you had to try so hard to hang on to them. And that struggle became part of who you are–part of what makes you worthy.

I want you to know that I get it. Stepping forward inevitably brings pain.

Maybe your pivot involves a friendship, a relationship that's been meaningful for years, but the step toward health and healing could lead to a disappointing outcome and you are afraid.

Perhaps your pivot is returning to work after years of being a stay-at-home mom. Parenting has changed you so much, and you're not sure that you're cut out for the workplace. And you're nervous that your "good mom points" will diminish once you're no longer one hundred percent available at home.

Or maybe you're moving. You feel a stirring to plant yourself somewhere else, but the decision presents the paralyzing prospect of moving you away from what you've always known. What if you leave and never fit in again?

Regardless of the circumstance or how it transpires, change can cultivate fear because we don't know exactly what is coming. And in most situations, just like mine, change threatens part of our identity.

This isn't a trivial experience. When something that makes us feel significant is at stake, we are vulnerable and cling to security, predictability, and sureness. Change means stepping into the unknown; and even if our "comfort zone" is unhealthy or toxic, it's frightening and overwhelming to move on.

Change is also painful. As Christians, we can buy into the lie that "if it's hard, it can't be God." I know I did. As much as I wanted all the disappointment, discouragement, and hardship to stop, the difficulty drew me near to Him. Like C.S. Lewis said, "He who has God and everything else has no more than he who has God only."

As you'll read in the chapters to come, "God only" was going to be my greatest discovery in this mandated pivot. Though releasing the church obligations seemed like what I wanted, it would not be easy.

I had found significance for twenty-five years inside those four walls called "church." But it was never good enough. And so, pain became God's megaphone to shatter my false ideas about significance. Pain makes God a necessity and "plants the white flag of truth within the fortress of the rebel soul."[1]

I didn't know it then, but I deeply craved this step of surrender. This would become my next step on the path of figuring out what really matters and would lead to a new level of understanding around this deep truth: I'm not defined by life's changes, challenges, success, or circumstances, but by my perspective as I line it up with a solid God.

As we'll explore, it can be really challenging for doers and achievers (ahem, present company included) to get this truth in our walk of faith. For many of us, thinking about what we want and envisioning what's ahead is easy and exciting, especially when it comes to mission and meaning. Doing our part in the process is rarely the issue—give us a goal and we'll make it happen. But beneath these mostly wonderful attributes lurks a tricky, sticky lie. Because achieving that has a big price tag. It's our worth.

What happens when God says, "let go"? When you believe that your significance is attached, letting go is the hardest thing to do.

---

[1] *Lewis, C. S. The Problem of Pain. Collins, 1957.*

"I'm not defined by life's changes, challenges, success, or circumstances, but by my perspective as I line it up with a solid God."

7

DO YOU WANT
TO BE HEALED?

There's a story in John chapter 5 about a man who was paralyzed and unable to walk. It says:

> "Inside the city, near the Sheep Gate, was the pool of Bethesda, with five covered porches. Crowds of sick people—blind, lame, or paralyzed—lay on the porches. One of the men lying there had been sick for thirty-eight years. When Jesus saw him and knew he had been ill for a long time, he asked him, 'Would you like to get well?'" John 5:2-6 NLT

It's an interesting question, "Would you like to get well?" Another translation of that passage poses the question this way, *"Do you want to be healed?"* Obviously, this man's affliction was physical, but that sentence got me thinking, do we really want to be healed? *Really?*

Maybe you do need physical healing. Or maybe you have a big dream or a deep desire for a rich relationship. Maybe you long for a healthy home. Regardless, I've learned over time that the healing and breakthrough we're seeking often requires deeper work. The deeper work that God is doing *in* you is preparation for the broader work He wants to do *through* you.

Confession: I don't particularly like the deeper work at first. In fact, sometimes the pain and heartache of my circumstances can hold me back from something new. In these instances, I need healing. And I must confront the broken areas in my heart with incredible intention to receive it.

> *The deeper work that God is doing in you is preparation for the broader work He wants to do through you.*

So, we return to Jesus' question because the same question He asked of the paralyzed man is the question He is asking us today.

Do you want to be healed?

Are you bitter from unforgiveness? Are you still broken from past loss or betrayal? Are you stuck hanging on to anger or disappointment with others? Maybe your angst is with God Himself? Do you want to get better?

The answer to these questions will bring clarity and end the spinning in your life. You will gain direction for *some* things but not *everything*. You will no longer be pining after the opportunities to be seen or approved. Your heart will be whole because it will be honest.

Don't settle for subpar. Don't ignore God's question—do you want to be healed?—just because it feels easier to stay frozen in your paralysis. Untreated wounds tend to get infected. Likewise, a broken heart left unattended often descends into bitterness. And bitterness can become a blanket that becomes strangely comfortable.

Do you want to get well? It can be easy to come up with excuses. I know I've always got a justified reason or two under my belt to help me procrastinate on taking my next step. The paralyzed man had his own set. Check out his response to Jesus in verse 7:

> *"I can't sir. For I have no one to put me into the pool when the water bubbles up. Someone else always gets there ahead of me." John 5:7 NLT*

"They did this to me."

"I don't have what it takes."

"It's just not possible given my circumstances."

When Jesus offered this man freedom, his excuses focused on the impossibilities. He was so consumed by what he could not do that he was unable to embrace the possibility of what God *could* do. He chose to blame others and focus on his limitations rather than lean into the solution staring him in the eye. All the man needed was Jesus. All the brokenness of his life didn't stand a chance against what God could do.

But he did what we often do: make excuses and blame others. The pain of changing can often seem greater than the pain of staying the same. And so, this man laid on his mat, literally looking his miracle square in the face.

What's staring you in the face? Are you fixing your eyes on circumstances or on the God who holds solutions in His hands? Have you become a victim—blaming others for your inability to move forward? Are you so consumed by what limits you that you cannot see the miracle right in front of you? This is what occurs when we look all around us and remove our eyes from what's possible with God.

It can be easier to focus on the problem than the promise. That's why Jesus asked the question. "Would you like to get well?" Put another way: "You want the problem or the promise?"

In verse 8, Jesus calls him up, "Stand up, pick up your mat, and walk!" I love how the Lord passionately pursued him. I love how He passionately pursues you and me. He has compassion for us, even in our wounded excuses. He gives one arms-wide-open opportunity after another to receive His restoration promise.

This guy had been sick for thirty-eight years. Thirty-eight years he had been lying on that mat. It had become his Unhappy Happy Place—his security blanket. His brokenness was really all he had ever known. His pain and limitation had become his comfort zone. It was *him*. So, Jesus' command to stand, pick it up, and walk was more than just a declaration of physical healing.

Jesus brought restoration to his whole outlook on life.

Jesus brought a challenge to surrender his false sense of security.

Jesus called him out of his comfort so that he could experience true confidence in Him.

On the everyday street corner of that man's struggle, God spoke the truth that His kids were born for more than broken.

There's a miracle staring at you in the face. And it's time to start gathering up the mats.

"It can be easier
to focus on
the problem
than the promise."

Section 2

IDENTITY

8

COMPARISON

As I sit here to write, I look up to see four old journals carefully stored in a glass cabinet with decorative items displayed in my living space.

It's a mystery to me why I have them on display.

I mean, I'm glad I saved them, but they ARE full of some of the most vulnerable confessions about myself. As I flip through the pages marked by years of prayers, musings, and gut-level honesty, I recognize one consistent theme *everywhere*. It's the thing that cuts to the core of what was always *really* going on inside my heart and head.

Can you guess what it is? It's *comparison*.

The stories in each journal are similar. Without fail, each dialogue starts with a dream and big hopes; there was no lack of high aspirations for me. This clear vision of what I wanted to create was always followed by a written prayer, defining my request to God in black and white. Finally, these prayers were backed up by Scripture, affirming and confirming the desire of my heart. In most situations, I knew what it would take and had even mapped out the actions. Line upon line expressed my dedication and commitment. It was written all over each page in ink.

And then it would begin to creep in, like a cold draft under the door: comparison.

How come HER, Lord? Why not me? If not yet, then when? Why aren't You delivering on MY behalf? What makes THEM better? I know You can do it for me, Lord, because You are doing it for them.

One of the stories that rang loud through the pages took place shortly after the writing of my first book. If you recall, I had just written *Thrive: Growing Through Life's Greatest Challenges* when our lives were shifted in a whole new direction. With so much unknown, I decided to do something with the work I had started and pitch what I had in my hands.

I googled the steps of putting together a press packet. I found a sample "letter to the publisher" and modified it to make sense for my context. I researched appropriate contacts and found addresses, ensuring that my packet would land on the right desk and not end up on some basement shelf. I stuffed each packet of my book to each editor with care. I added a selection of a few of my best writings–the ones that all my family and closest friends had commented on, admired, and said made a difference. I submitted a handwritten note "to whom it may concern" just to add a personal touch.

I was proud, excited, and certain. Certain that this could be it. Inside those oversized manilla envelopes were the keys to my success. With each postage stamp, I was sealing the deal for my future. I snapped a quick pic at the post office to boldly share the news with my social network–proof-positive that this small beginning was about to explode into something great.

And then.... nothing. Yep! That's correct. After six months of waiting for a response, I had heard nothing. I think it's safe to say the answer was "no."

Rejection. Denial. The basement shelf. Not even a note in response.

No copy/paste email to let me down gently. No formal letter just to express their disinterest. Nope. Nothing. When I acknowledged that my writings were not accepted, I reverted to my go-to emotion when my expectations weren't met—*anger*. Licking my wounds, I got real snarky about publishers and the many ministries I had submitted my work to.

"You can't reject me. I reject YOU!" my insecurity spewed out.

And then came the comparison. I had good friends with less experience than me, and with no effort, they received contracts and big deals with publishing companies. Worse, I knew a few women who didn't even do the work of pursuing publishers but scored a deal anyway. They were pursued out of nowhere, and opportunity fell in their lap. I'd even worked with, ministered alongside, and *led* some of these other writers who had been fortuitously accepted by these companies.

Why them and not me? I mused. *How come it's their turn? And more importantly, when will it be mine? I did the work. I put in the effort. I authored the book with four babies in tow and now was in a heap of excruciating transitions. God, why, at the very least, can't You throw me a bone?*

These questions became a steady drumbeat in my journal pages. My dashed expectations were flooded with unfiltered emotion, made even more grievous by the comparison that would rise and threaten to take me out.

Going back over my old journals, it's clear so many of my expectations were not only derailed or denied; *they were fulfilled for someone else.* Sometimes it was a stranger. But so often it was someone close to me. I was happy for her. I could genuinely congratulate her. I could even *celebrate* her. But also, I was just so overwhelmed with how sad I was *for myself.*

These journal entries are so clear. My tendency to compare was the primary action that haunted me most. Comparison was the story on repeat no matter the occasion.

Page upon page, project upon project, season upon season, comparison would rear its ugly head and I would compete. This time it stared me in the face when I could have been honored, but comparison humiliated me. Maybe you can relate.

> *Comparison was the story on repeat no matter the occasion.*

Every October, I was invited to attend an advanced leadership summit for my business. Held annually in the beautiful mountains of Sundance, Utah, its intent was to gather the highest levels of coaching leadership in a retreat-style format for personal development, strategic planning, and continued growth. It was an honor to be invited. I had to reach ranking qualifications to go and looked forward to attending every year.

Being invited obviously indicated that I had found *some* success in my company. Many people would have given anything to be included. People worked diligently year after year to qualify for this event, and I was no exception. I had done it. Some might even have said that I'd arrived.

But I didn't feel that. Even with challenging work and great achievement, I was not satisfied. I had an insatiable appetite for significance. And even after our tumultuous struggle had stabilized, the cycle of longing for success still stirred in my heart.

This mode of operation often moved me out of my lane of purpose, robbing me of all contentment and putting me in a place of competition. It would come in waves. One of those waves crashed over me during this Sundance event. I sat in my seat as one of my colleagues took the stage. His introduction was full of accolades and achievements. He had experienced incredible success and was racing to the top. He was running his race in business. And he ran right past me.

I should be first, I thought begrudgingly. He started *after* me. On the tail of these jealous thoughts came suspicion, even accusation. I'm not proud of this, but I even found myself making up a story in my mind about how he got a leg up, as if his circumstances gave him unearned privilege: *He's favored by the company. He has it easy. He isn't juggling the situations I face.*

From accusation I then moved on to self-bullying: *Jen, what are you missing? You must work harder. You still aren't good enough. Maybe it's time to just quit.*

Nice, right?

I'm not a quitter, so naturally I went to my full belt of tools to flip the script on my self-talk: *Jen, take these thoughts captive. Celebrate his success. Stop comparing; it's robbing your joy.* But even with the personal pep talk, I still wrestled. I needed to prove myself worthy through external achievements. And the root of my striving was planted deep. It was as though I needed surgery to cut it out.

My focus was rarely solely on "her" or "him." It was most often on me. Some days were better than others, but far too often comparisons just crashed my party like an uninvited guest, intruding on my rather good life. I had a loving family, an incredibly caring husband, and good friends. Most would consider me successful, and I lived my life to please God. Yet, almost every day, comparison would nudge its way into my life. The temptation to compare would creep up...

...with a passing comment on my Instagram feed

...through a brief text or even when I chopped my hair to add some spunk.

...when I'd say no to this party, but yes to that dinner.

...when I'd pack my kids' lunches or not allow them to get iPhones.

...when I'd speak the truth or create relationship boundaries.

...when I'd say no or when I'd say yes.

The amount of energy I spent looking to the left and the right was beyond exhausting–it had become paralyzing.

For instance, I would find myself scrolling on Facebook and come across a writer who was better than me. (It wasn't that hard. Of course, there are better writers than me out there. I'm a simple author with a well-designed blog. I know the facts and understand my reality.) But I'd read her new post about her book, and the abundance of comments from people praising her work would cause my heart to sink. (As though somehow there just aren't enough positive comments in the world to go around.) And then the fears of worthlessness and insignificance would flood in. Fears that led straight to self-bullying.

"You'll never be good enough," I punked myself. "Who do you think you are? What do *you* really have to say anyway? Nobody cares. You're kidding yourself."

Ever felt that way?

Jealousy would ooze from deep within, like a contagion feeding on fear, competition, and self-protection. Coveting someone else's success would lead to feeling ugly, uninvited, and like a complete failure. Turns out, coveting never really goes the way I want it to.

And to think, this nasty flood of comparison would all come from one, measly, harmless online post.

I knew that my feelings were not facts. In fact, I spent much of my work and ministry trying to help others see this for themselves. Yet I was consistently allowing my emotions to fester, convincing my mind of a fateful nightmare story about who I was.

I also knew that copying, competing, and comparing would lead to burnout. But still...I would scroll through the feed of Instagram profiles and wonder, *how much "stranger influence" can I gain?*

If likes and follows were up, so was I. If they were down, then I was, too.

In my heart of hearts, I knew this striving and comparison was wrong. But fear of insignificance drove me. And it drove me hard. One minute I wondered, *why can't I simply serve an audience of one? Why am I cheapening my purpose for a pretty version of striving?* And in the next minute I would protest, *Why won't you just do this for me, Lord? Why can't I win? Why are you elevating her, while I'm over here in her dust?*

It's not pretty, right? But the comparison trap is just that—a trap.

Here's the thing: Comparison is a worthiness issue. It's a snare expertly placed by the Enemy of our souls. Comparison causes us to doubt, diminish, and deny the goodness of God in us. The truth is we were created in the image of Christ Jesus, the image of the King. As His kids, we are chosen and set apart. We're royalty! But comparison makes us start acting like paupers and pretenders, causing us to fall into the abyss of jealousy and rivalry. Comparison makes us forget who we are.

The moment we decide to follow Jesus, we become joint heirs in His kingdom. He places and shapes our passions and desires. But we lose sight of this truth when we are off looking at someone else. We lose sight of it being about *Him and us.*

"One of the biggest battles you'll have to face every single day of your life is the battle to stay focused on what you've been called to do, and not get distracted by what anyone else is doing. It takes great humility and strength to stay in your lane."—Christine Caine

"Comparison causes us to _doubt_, _diminish_, and _deny_ the goodness of God in us."

There is no one-size-fits-all version of who and what matters. When we demand some prototype of significance—of what matters, or of who is good or right, or of how big or small or loud or soft or fast or slow—when we compare ourselves to the mythical "him" or "her," it is a detriment to the entire community. We are all wired on purpose *for a purpose*. Mega is not a greater value. Modest is not less.

I got out of the comparison trap one healthier step at a time. And it began with the harsh reality that my desire for more had me thinking and believing less. There was no abundance in my mindset. It was rooted in lack. Comparison had me trapped with a focus on what others were doing, preventing me from the fullness of what God was asking me to do.

I had to begin to recognize more clearly the voice of my adversary that seeks to "steal, kill and destroy." And when you speak the truth, you shame the enemy, which was part of my path out.

I created a list on the pages of my journals moving forward that declared who God says I am. For every "why not, how come, if only, what about me?" statement, I replaced it with "I am, He says, it will, and so be it." God has given all His children, including me, unique gifts to use for His glory. And in His house, there is room for ALL of us. *She* is not my competition; *she* is my sister in the Lord. Furthermore, *she* is proof it can be done.

God showed me in His goodness that there are no limits to His blessings. Again, I saw lack when His promise is abundance. There is room for all of us to feast at the table. The resources of God are unlimited. He is not short on opportunities, blessings, or wins. I began to see the good work with the unique gifts of others build my faith instead of causing me to doubt my abilities. Their success was proof that it could be done. And if God can do it for them, He can do it for us too. He is completing a good work in us and through us.

There is a passage in Ephesians 4:1 when Paul is imprisoned, urging us, the reader, to walk worthy of the calling we have received. When I looked up the opposite of worthy, the word that appears is *nothing*. Not a blank page, but the literal word: *nothing*.

> *When He is filling my cup, I will always have plenty to pour out.*

I am not nothing, and neither are you. We are God's masterpiece. We are His children; we are heirs of the King. But my comparison trap led me down this dark road that led me to believe I was *nothing*. When, the God of the universe, Creator of all things, says I'm *worthy*.

What's *your* design? What's *your* preference? What's *your* dream, *your* personality?

Now's your chance to stop comparing yourself to *him* or *her*—feeling like an imposter. It's time to take your rightful place in full confidence.

"So that you may walk worthy of the Lord, fully pleasing to Him: bearing fruit in every good work and growing in the knowledge of God." Colossians 1:10 CSB

Here's the thing: I may not have all I want (yet). But when I see it in the life of another, I don't have to fear that I will miss out. I will give to, encourage, support, and applaud the gift someone else has been given.

In the Kingdom of God, there is no power struggle; there is a powerful union. There is no lack, only abundance. If I want to receive, then I must willingly give. This is the generous nature of Jesus. And as a follower of His, I can be generous even amid my own need. When He is filling my cup, I will always have plenty to pour out.

Here is my hope for you as you combat comparison. Instead of comparing, start celebrating those around you and praising God for allowing them to be where they are today.

Next time you feel comparison and doubt creeping in, congratulate or encourage the person who is accomplishing a good thing and becoming who God created them to be.

This is your practical act of surrender. This will help you to take your eyes off your own defeat and see the win of another as something good. It is a daily surrender. It is living out the command in Exodus 20:17 that we should not covet our neighbor's house or anything else our neighbor has.

When we compare, we are telling God that we don't trust the plans He has for us. And so, as we walk out our obedience to the instruction of God, we are placing our hopes in His hands. When we compare ourselves to others in an unhealthy way, we desire what others have instead of trusting God with what He's given us.

When you find yourself in the comparison trap, call it out. We find freedom from comparison when we confess it. This is why my journal had pages of heartache scribbled in ink. But giving these moments to God in written form disabled them from being stuck in my heart and enabled healing and truth to take root in their place.

I urge you to confess and ask God for forgiveness. As you find freedom from wanting another person's story, ask God for strength to trust Him in yours. There is a beautiful story being written in and through your life.

As comparison creeps in, start saying, "God, I trust you. I trust you." This can be a battle in your mind or audible words you speak aloud wherever you find yourself. Shift your focus to God and begin to thank Him, knowing that even when you can't see it, He's working, and you will not be left out.

9

FEAR OF INSIGNIFICANCE

I remember the days when my children were little like they were yesterday. Those days ran like clockwork. No matter how early or how late they were put to bed, the wake-up call was consistent and the same.

Moms, you know what I'm talking about: the cycle of eat, play, sleep, *repeat* went on and on. I considered myself a real expert when I was able to get three out of the four kids in the same naptime routine. Even their meals were on a rotation of yogurt, bananas, sweet potatoes, mac 'n cheese, spaghetti, and our weekly Wednesday adventures to Chick-Fil-A.

I have precious memories from that time. Priceless. But I would also clearly define it as *a very mundane season*. Fortunately, God, in His goodness, would speak to me in the middle of bath time or folding tiny little onesies. He never neglected to bring encouragement to the monotony that sometimes made for a heavy heart.

It was during that season that I began to take notes on my laptop after the kids went to bed. I would journal my thoughts upright in bed while I waited for my husband to get home from his long hours at work.

One late night he arrived home and caught me typing tirelessly in our bed. His curiosity was piqued as he glanced over my shoulder to see my work. "Maybe you should write a book," he said. He saw the words I was typing and thought they would be valuable to others.

I had never considered myself much of a writer. My digital journal was just a place to process, giving me a voice in the middle of my mundane. But that late-night suggestion sparked a new possibility. And in the months that followed, I went to work writing and publishing my first book. That was a decade ago and *a lot* of life has happened since then. But I still remember the hope that was in my heart as I typed on that laptop. What started as a passion project quickly became my ticket to purpose. In the back of my mind, there was a thought that maybe this was it.

Somewhere between journaling on a laptop late at night and stringing my words all together in the form of a book, I discovered a drive to see something put me on the map.

My expectations were disappointed because the book did not put me on the map in the way I'd hoped. In spite of watching the success of others in publishing, my book didn't launch me into the influential stratosphere I'd dreamed of. As I said, I wrestled with comparison, anger, and angst; but that wasn't all. Beneath these reactions lurked something even deeper—a fear I'd carried for nearly my whole life.

I was <u>afraid</u> of being <u>insignificant</u>. And God wanted to <u>liberate</u> me.

I remember an early encounter with the feeling of insignificance. It's where everyone starts perfecting their feelings of insignificance: junior high. Mine happened in a middle school bathroom stall.

"I was _afraid_ of being _insignificant_. And God wanted to _liberate_ me."

A bit of backstory: I was a church kid, and in the '80s at my church, kids' musicals were a thing. A big deal, actually. This worked out surprisingly well for me because I *loved* the stage. I auditioned for any part and often got the lead.

That is until middle school. I remember sitting in the church pew, waiting for the casting announcements. I assumed—we all assumed—they were going to say Jenny Nicks (that was me) for the starring role.

But instead, it was someone else.

Another eighth-grade girl had beaten me out. After the announcement was made, in my disappointment, I made my way to the bathroom, taking refuge in the first empty stall. Not long after, my new rival and another friend walked in, excited about the casting announcement and unaware that I was *also* there—behind door number one.

"Can you believe it?" she said. "I finally beat out Jenny!" This victory cheer was followed by lots of giggles and a few cutdowns in between.

These girls were supposed to be my "friends." We had known each other since toddler Sunday school. And they were Christians on top of it. The cutting words and competition struck right at my self-worth, causing my heart to sink as I sat silently in that bathroom stall.

Looking back, that was a big moment for me. Maybe you have a similar experience–a moment of feeling insignificant. What has shaped your sense of self-worth? Remember that one episode that really hurt you—shaped you? Do you remember where you were and how it felt? Who was there and what did they say?

Most importantly, what did you learn? For me, I learned a few lessons in that bathroom stall that have lingered with me for a lifetime:

* People want to be close to me until they don't, until they feel threatened, and I am misunderstood.

* I learned that I am both loved and despised for my strengths and my gifts.

* I learned to suck it up. Be fine. At the end of the day, nobody is truly safe.

* I learned about exclusion and began my search for belonging. Where did I fit if my own circle was willing to cut me out?

* I learned to prove it. Prove you can manage the pain. Prove you can be kind; just turn the other cheek. Prove your worth. Do more, achieve more, and perform. *That's what people admire about you, Jenny. You're significant when you're a star.*

* I learned to please the crowd. You will be mocked, betrayed, misunderstood, and misrepresented no matter what you do. But please them just the same.

* I learned to double down through striving and controlling. "I WILL matter. I MUST. I have something to prove."

Ever learned a few lessons in a junior high bathroom stall? My location may have been different than yours, but I'm betting you have your own list of life lessons. Lessons hard learned in pain, and whose bitter after-taste has a way of lingering long into adulthood. Feelings of insignificance can start young, but they don't age well.

Ultimately, I stepped out of that stall and said, "Hi, girls. Congratulations." I walked out with my head high, but I'd been changed. Those lessons were *not* a good education. And they stuck. In that bathroom stall, I had made agreements with the Enemy of my soul to buy into a lie about my true significance.

That lie was that significance came from my performance. I had to earn it, succeed for it, become influential for it, strive for it.

From that point on, I started striving for approval and became desperate for accolades. This angst became my normal. I looked at the size of my Instagram following. I measured the response of my readers. I calculated how much I was loved by my growing platform. My worth was established by the next big thing.

The more affirmation I received from others, the more my sense of significance grew. I scrambled, I hustled. I could *not* lose, I had to earn. Striving was my method of mattering. It was the way I could determine if my life would count.

This was the mentality that drove me to succeed in my health coaching business. Could I grow it bigger? Could I make more money? Could I get more approval? Could I be recognized as the top? I inscribed every page of my journals with my commitment to get ahead, no matter what. And guess what? It worked! I was thriving—earning more than I'd ever thought possible, buying a new house, and leading a team.

Sometimes the things we're good at are the very things holding us captive. My hustle mentality, rooted in the lie that significance was mine to earn, was particularly sinister because it fit so neatly into the world's formula for success. I am ambitious, goal-oriented, and confident—qualities that naturally drew admiration, reinforcing the performance cycle. It was easy for me to press onward with my striving because I saw so many others doing–and praising–exactly the same thing.

But also...it had a dark side. Though I was in many ways successful, it was also easy to feel like I was consistently coming up short. It picked at my worthiness when my kids were struggling or the church was floundering. It poked at my sense of security, whispering to me that if I quit striving, the bottom would drop out.

No matter what I achieved or how fast I achieved it, even my work didn't feel like it was enough. Everything felt like it needed to be exponential. Exponential people. Exponential impact. Exponential growth. I pined after anything and everything exponential. I wanted people to admire me. I wanted people to see me for my sacrifice and abundance.

My deepest desire was to be significant. But the flipside was my greatest fear: that my life wouldn't count. I was constantly looking for validation through all my accomplishments, which left me incredibly vulnerable if those accomplishments, or the applause they generated, faltered in any way. Because the applause of others was the source of my worth.

And so we come full circle: me, seeking applause in the starring role, yet finding myself heartbroken in a bathroom stall. Don't we all find ourselves in the bathroom stall at one time or another, seeking significance but then having our self-worth swirl down the drain?

Maybe it was on the first day of a new job and the fear of failure left you stowed away, escaping the terror. Maybe the bathroom has become your great escape from the kids, your spouse, or the sketchy uncle at family gatherings. Maybe you ran to the stall to find confidence as you braved a new adventure, hoping that you have what it takes to succeed.

Whether you find yourself in the bathroom stall questioning who you are or deciding who you will become, I get it. It's been decades since that bathroom stall, and I'm still unlearning the lessons I learned there.

My path to the truth about significance unfolded during the very season that I described at the start of this book. I was pushing in my journal pages to keep hustling, keep pressing in; but God was shouting from the rooftops that my worth was not in what I could do.

The suffering that had tormented me since my early years in a bathroom stall was not the life He had for me. His hope for my future was not rooted in my ability to succeed, my years of collecting trophies, and my attempts to be number one. Hope for my future was rooted in HIM.

Slowly, I began to hear that truth from God. It was starting to sink in that my Savior's love and His prosperous plan ahead were not established on my performance. God had to teach me what significance and influence really were. It's not about what we do. It's about whose we are.

I'll never forget a phone conversation I had with a friend during this season when the truth about significance finally began to sink in. As we said goodbye, the last words out of my mouth were, "Make it happen!" Immediately I wanted to call back and apologize. Not because the words were offensive. Not because they were even bad. Taking action is good! But I recognized that I was projecting my own need to succeed onto her.

> It's not about what we do. It's about whose we are.

It really doesn't matter what you do for work. Whether you run a large company, or stay home full-time to raise a family, the mantra ringing loud and strong through our culture is "MAKE IT HAPPEN! Keep that nose to the grindstone and get it done."

Perhaps you live by a similar motto and keep spinning on the hamster wheel to success. However, when we force the pace of the rat race, like it or not, we will eventually get run over. This is why I wanted to call my friend back. This is what I was sorry about.

By this point, you might be asking yourself, "What's wrong with wanting to make an impact?" And the answer is simple: there is nothing innately wrong with wanting to succeed and make an impact. But when the outcomes of your work become your idol, it's time to put your heart in check. Whatever we treasure more than God, whatever drives our thoughts and actions, becomes an idol. And these idols dull our spiritual hearing and harden our hearts to things of God.

Having grown up in church as a child, it was challenging to wrap my mind around the reality that I might have any idols. My picture of an idol was the golden calf that I saw in a picture book in Sunday School class many years before. But as Tim Keller states, "an idol is anything more important to you than God, anything that absorbs your heart and imagination more than God, and anything that you seek to give you what only God can give."[2]

As I leaned into the discomfort of my own emotions during this season, I began to understand that an idol can be anything that takes the place of God as the most important focus and priority in our life. The modern-day idol has become whatever feeds the flesh, brings comfort and security, and is pursued in the place of our passion for God. Idols are dangerous substitutes for God as the primary foundation of our lives.

Take, for instance, the casual question we ask each other when we're meeting for the first time, "So, what do you do?" When we are enslaved by the idol of success, this simple question can elicit one of two reactions: insecurity or pride. Either way, we soon find ourselves listing all our accomplishments in an effort to prove our worth or gain respect. But God measures success based on obedience, not results. In all things, our role is to obey; He's responsible for the outcome.

When we're looking at the world's definitions of influence, impact, and success, it's easy to get caught up by the "glamor": the shoes, the glossy photos, the viral videos, and the whole dog-and-pony-show. We begin to think, oh this is IT. This is where it's at.

"It" is the highlight reel. It's the moments in life that feel far out there; but if we can attain them, we'll find fulfillment. It's the stage for some, the backstage for others. It's the occasion for the sequins

[2] Keller, Timothy. Counterfeit Gods: The Empty Promises of Money, Sex, and Power, and the Only Hope That Matters. Riverhead Books, 2011.

on a runway or the new boots for the top of that mountain. It's the promotion you longed for, the deal you just sealed. These days, it's the video that's gone viral.

Pick your poison, name your fame, these are the "it" moments we're often waiting for.

But that's not at all what Scripture tells us about the Kingdom of God and what defines "it." And just like anything of earthly value, it will pass, and it will not satisfy.

Believe me, I know.

I have gone viral. I have been on stages in stadiums with thousands of people. It is fun. It's a thrill. And it lasts about as long as fifteen seconds of a viral video. I have never been more convinced of the truth that happiness, joy, and contentment are not generated by achievement.

The satisfaction from outward success is fleeting. In fact, living in this need for viral is often a malicious cause of suffering. If you don't get what you want, you suffer. If you get what you don't want, you suffer. Even when you do get exactly what you want, you still suffer because you can't hold on to it forever. Real significance is an inside job.

"Actually, I don't have a sense of needing anything personally. I've learned by now to be quite content whatever my circumstances. I'm just as happy with little as with much, with much as with little. I've found the recipe for being happy whether full or hungry, hands full or hands empty. Whatever I have, wherever I am, I can make it through anything in the One who makes me who I am." Phil 4:11-13 MSG

When we take our cues from this letter from Paul, then the life we have, regardless of its highs and lows, offers joy. This is "it." It is not something *out there*.

Attaching your happiness to your achievements causes suffering. If you believe you're nothing without your status, position, wealth, or awards, when someone outshines you in the marketplace, your opinion of yourself will drop. Conditional happiness puts your self-perception at the whim of someone else's experience.

Our desire for significance in this false sense can take us off mission. Learn from others, but don't let your desire for influence cause you to do things that are "it" for you. Do not pursue success. Pursue Jesus instead. Then, your business, your ministry and even your viral video will bring sparks of joy into your life. But they were never meant to be *the source*. That's God's job.

I recently found myself in another bathroom. I was backstage in a large arena this time. I stepped into the stall just one last time before I walked out onto the platform. This time I was not getting ready for a church middle school play performance. This time it was the middle-aged me stepping onto a stage as me. All of me.

As I stood for one last glance and faced the mirror, I snapped a selfie. It was one of those moments you post to social media because it holds a lot of meaning. (Or maybe you don't, because it's a moment just between you and that face in the mirror.) Regardless, for me, these were the thoughts that went through my head as I stared head-on, eyeball to eyeball with my reflection. I said to myself, audibly in a soft whisper, "You're not that eighth-grade girl anymore. You have nothing to prove, only something to give."

It was there, in that new bathroom, that I strongly disagreed with the Enemy of my soul. He had hijacked too many moments since that first bathroom stall. His attempt to deceive me and hold me back with a twisted truth was no longer effective. I was closing the door on his lies.

I was significant with nothing to prove. Only something to give.

10

APPROVAL ADDICTION

Abe Lincoln famously said, "You can please all of the people some of the time, and you can please some of the people all of the time, but you can't please all of the people all of the time."

We have a cultural norm: it's the contrived virtue of pleasing people. It's coupled with the fear that we'll let people down. And so, we frequently say yes when we should say no. Often this habit comes from a desire to avoid the pain of rejection and to prove ourselves worthy.

In many cases, this drive to please can be rooted in a need to belong. We were created as social beings, to live in community with one another. So it's normal to want to fit in and belong. God placed this longing within the human heart to draw us closer to Him and one another—to help us experience the same oneness that God the Father, Son and Holy Spirit have with one another.

The problem arises when we place our desire for people to like us *above* our relationship with God. Failing to obey when overcome by the fear of what others might think, whether speaking truth or reaching out to the marginalized, means we've fallen into the trap of idolatry. In valuing people's approval more than God's, we demonstrate where our true loyalties lie. Jesus put it this way in Matthew 6:24: "No one can serve two masters. Either you will hate the one and love the other, or you will be devoted to the one and despise the other."

I come by my desire to please others, and its accompanying problems, honestly. (Maybe you do, too.) For instance, a while back, I bought myself a new car. Cars aren't really the kind of thing that gets me excited in life—I'm not a "car person." So, on the one hand, this was just a car for me. But also...it was a *really nice* car. Luxurious, even. And I bought it myself from the income I was earning in my business, which was fun and exciting.

I was extremely thankful for this car. But with it came a lot of people-pleasing angst. You see, I was afraid of judgment from people who believed that I should not have nice things as a follower of Christ. This is the "What Would Mother Teresa Drive?" kind of question.

Now, by no means am I attempting to paint Christians with a broad brush and suggest everyone who believes in God or goes to church thinks this way. But it's a mindset that some people have, and it was one I had picked up along the way, too. As I stared at my car in the garage, a little voice whispered, "You should be focused on *giving* big, not buying big." "Enjoying this car is shameful." "It's going *without* that breeds humility and brings me closer to Jesus, not material gain." And so on.

My mindset around money was something that God had been dealing with in me. He often reminded me that money is just money—it's neither good nor bad. It's *the love* of it that is the root of all evil.

And I don't *love* money. I love God and I love people. Furthermore, when money is in the hands of people who put Him first, good things can happen to resource His work.

I was growing into these truths about money, but still—those whispered thoughts of shame stirred up all kinds of anxiety about my new luxury car. A big part of me just wanted to hide it from the world—not let anyone know that I'd bought it. I decided to resist this impulse; and in a feeble attempt to overcome my fear of needing people's approval in this area of my life, I decided to share about it on social media.

As you might expect, most people were kind. Many extended words of encouragement and celebrated with me. But then came...the pushback. One person had strong opinions about me. She accused me of being a phony—someone who talks about Jesus and acts as though her life is in line with Him yet buys herself a fancy car. *Jesus was born in a stable, you know.* She accused my faith of being false—that somehow, I had lost my true north of what true happiness was because I'd bought myself this car.

It was just an opinion, but it hurt. Her words impacted precisely at one of the most tender spots in my life's story.

> *I don't love money.*
> *I love God and*
> *I love people.*

I was constantly carrying the weight of magnifying glasses pointed in my direction, anticipating the moment I would fail other people's "litmus test." Was I measuring up? Were my efforts good enough? Was I meeting their expectations of how I should think, act, look, and live?

These questions were wearing me out. I found myself doing things out of obligation so that "they" would think I was great. Even worse, my own internal critic had the loudest voice and the most demanding examination.

I'm sure you have a similar inner critic, lurking in the shadows, poking at you constantly. Mine has been in my life for forty-some-odd years. Sometimes she whispers. Sometimes she screams. Some days are better than others. She's rarely welcome, but she doesn't seem to care. She barges in just about everywhere I go. In the things that matter most, most would consider me successful. And I live my life to please God. Yet, almost every day I have a combative conversation with *her*.

When I pair those shoes with that dress.

When I say no to this gathering, but yes to that dinner.

When I do videos with my kids or press send on that post.

When I speak the truth or create relationship boundaries.

When I say no or when I say yes.

Each time I wonder, *what is she going to think?*

Your "she" is different from mine. But I'm betting that "she" haunts you, too. "She" is what other people think. And all too often, "she" holds us back and paralyzes us in fear.

"She" is the personification of my approval addiction. And I needed to let go of her. So do you.

While sensitivity to the needs of others is appropriate, being *consumed* by the *opinions* of others is not. It's an unhealthy path God never intended for us to walk.

"The Lord is my helper; I will not fear; what can man do to me?" Hebrews 13:6 NKJV

We can be affected by the opinions of other people, but we don't have to be *directed* by them. Inevitably we are going to be touched by the thoughts and judgments of others—it's going to show up in our life from time to time—but we don't have to allow it to control us, consume us, or conform us to the thoughts and values of others.

People are vital to our existence. But they're just that: *people*. Because they're just people, we don't put our *faith* in them. We don't entrust

"While sensitivity to the needs of others is appropriate, being consumed by the opinions of others is not."

our future to their opinions or allow them to rule our lives. Instead, we focus on how God sees us. We fix our eyes on His truth and let Him lead our lives.

"Let the favor of the Lord our God be upon us;
And confirm for us the work of our hands;
Yes, confirm the work of our hands." Psalm 90:17 NASB1995

Did you catch that first line of verse seventeen? He favors you! Favor is an attitude of approval. *He approves of you,* which means that the approval of others is not only not necessary but also irrelevant.

You have a supreme destiny—crafted by the Lord your God. You are the handiwork of Someone bigger and greater and more glorious than you can possibly imagine. And He built you for something bigger and greater than you can possibly imagine (Ephesians 3:20). That's what He thinks about you. That's His ambition toward you. So, on the days when the thoughts of others are piercing your ears and clanging around loudly in your head, fix your heart toward your Creator and hear what He has already said.

This is what I hear. See if you can hear it too:

* I am loved
* I am forgiven
* My past does not define me
* I am not what others say about me
* I am not my diagnosis
* I am not my failings or my weakness
* My past, my hurt, my hang-ups, and my setbacks will either grow me or diminish me. I will be bold and choose growth.

If we are going to live a life of significance, we have to let go of the need to be admired by all and to live solely for an audience of One.

I've let go of comparison and worrying about what others might think I should do or what I should drive. I have trusted that while it is my responsibility to pick up my mat, He is the One who empowers my walk. He opens doors that no one can shut.

I cannot go to all the places I need to go, nor can I say all the things I need to say if I go at this life without Him. Neither can you. So, when I am distracted by others' opinions, He keeps me rooted. When I question, He gives me perspective. When I am weak, He is able to do miracles beyond my strength.

Of course, we do have a part to play in people's lives. God's plan for us always includes one another. We are a grand display of God's purposes lived out loud. But pleasing the crowd isn't the goal. I realized that the road of living to please Him alone was going to stretch me. To live undistracted by the disapproval or approval of others sounded so peaceful yet painful all at once. But it was time to do something different. It was time to walk worthy.

This new walk of worthy meant that I would begin to judge my success by God's standards. I could no longer look to the number of followers on Instagram to determine my influence. I had to stop judging my mothering against the mom next door and what she was doing for her kids. It was time to appreciate my body in its aging process and continue my path toward health despite whomever may disagree or disapprove.

So, could I be okay with His approval being enough?

This question is a tricky one. But deep in my heart the answer was, yes! I wanted to be okay with Him alone. The thought of this new way of living began to bring relief. If I set Him as my standard, then even if what I set my hands to does not work out the way that I hope, my significance is not at stake. Because my significance in Jesus is never based on what I do.

I'm significant (and so are you) because of who Jesus says you ARE. So, in the end, my success will be based on a higher standard. One that is agreed upon between the Lord and me. And this brought tremendous peace.

I can do that.

It was time to reject the idea that my value was based on the external validations of others or my inner critic. The burden of winning, excelling, appeasing, and always succeeding was heavy; and I was tired of carrying it.

> *I'm significant (and so are you) because of who Jesus says you ARE.*

The car I drive. How much money I make. The way my kids perform. The size of my jeans. The circle I'm connected to. The size of my church. The next big thing, the next dream. Constantly running all of these things, plus more, through the "litmus test" of external approval was a burden.

In Matthew 11:28, Jesus asks, "Are you weary, carrying a heavy burden?" So often my answer was YES. Yes Lord, I am! But notice that He doesn't stop there:

> *"Then come to me. I will refresh your life, for I am your oasis. Simply join your life with mine. Learn my ways and you'll discover that I'm gentle, humble, easy to please. You will find refreshment and rest in me. For all that I require of you will be pleasant and easy to bear."—Matthew 11:28-30*

This rest and refreshment were the life that I desired. I wanted my kids to see me dream and work toward good things. But the thought of my children's foundational memories being of how Mom was always striving and pursuing some unattainable need for fulfillment because she was wrestling with her purpose brought me to my knees.

This passage from Matthew, this promise of rest, meant that dream-chasing could be freed from the longing for worth, approval, or validation. Sure, it was still work, still structure, still collaboration, still time and resources. But the effort came from a place of wholeness instead of hustle. It could become an easy overflow of who I was and what God had done in me.

This promise from Jesus also gave me permission to enjoy my journey and focus my attention on the ones who brought me joy—the people who mattered most. There would be seasons when my influence would be greatest (and most precious) with the toes around my table. I no longer felt pressure to reach the masses with influencer status; I could rest in being an influencer of four. This was the refreshing my soul needed and a burden that was light.

Where do you need some permission to enjoy the journey? Where could your focus sharpen up? Who are the ones that bring you the greatest joy? Who are the toes around your table?

Sometimes we just need a moment to recalibrate, to reset. Sometimes we need a minute to remember what matters most and lean into it. One of my great desires in writing this book is that you would have a moment of clarity—perhaps a word of challenge and encouragement you can relate to—that causes you to align your life in a new, healthier way.

There is no doubt your soul could use some refreshing. There is no question your heart could use a load lifted. Every person I've ever met is in that boat. I'm just here to remind you that you have a compassionate Creator—a loving Lord—who stands ready to re-write your story as you have known it, to redeem your past, and to restore hope for your future. He stands ready to do something divinely different in your life right this very instant. And to set your life on significance in Him.

11

IMPOSTER SYNDROME

I'd been invited to an event with an amazing circle of accomplished women who were full of faith and success. These were high-achieving businesswomen who were using their savvy to support others and build God's Kingdom. They had embraced me into their community; and as it turned out, they also had their Gucci on.

On the one hand, I felt like I belonged. I was full of faith. I had a business. I was all about building God's Kingdom. On the other hand, I was newer to the business world; church ministry had been my whole life. I was driving an older model Toyota Rav4. I didn't own Gucci *anything*. I had seen some success in my small pond but nothing like they had with all the zeros at the end of their paychecks.

This event was only an hour's drive up the Pacific Coast Highway— the ocean to the left, great coffee shops, cute boutiques, and the finest restaurants to the right. This was my city, and I belonged here.

But as I neared the turn into the Ritz Carlton at Laguna Niguel, I began to tell myself a different story. I pulled into the valet with my Toyota Rav4; and as the kind gentleman asked me if I was checking in, all I heard was, "You don't belong here."

I immediately panicked. I was about to valet my car with its empty bag of Skinny Pop and can of Bubbly water on the front passenger seat. And I had no cash for the tip. With confidence I didn't feel, I replied, "Yes, thank you, and would you mind grabbing my bags please?" Except, of course, for my small crossbody Louis Vuitton. I'd carry that one by myself, thank you very much.

I knew the crowd I was about to immerse myself in and was relieved to have at least one item that would communicate that I could fit in here, too. As I waited in the short line at the check-in desk, I sized up the girl in front of me from head to toe. I identified every designer she wore because I'm kind of into all of that. I had her outfit totaling thousands of dollars and that was just the shoes and bag she carried her small puppy in.

"It's fine, I'm fine. But I'm going straight to my room," I said to myself.

I entered a lovely ocean-view room with a plush king-sized bed covered in luxurious white linens. I turned the corner to find the most glorious bathroom. It was *next level.* I opened the door to see the white robes carefully hung. As they draped properly to the ground, I saw the plush white slippers ready and waiting for my convenience and comfort. I stepped into a smaller closed-off space where I found the toilet. It was my first experience with a seat you could warm.

I felt like royalty. I wanted to capture it—to be still in this time and this space. Silly as it sounds, I was enamored by the room you go potty in. I stopped, looked straight in the mirror, and did the natural thing: I took a selfie.

And then it all hit me.

Who are you kidding? You don't really belong here. You are not like these ladies. You don't make that kind of cash. You don't have as much success. You aren't even prepared to tip the bellman bringing up your bags. These women are brilliant. They are true entrepreneurs. They have created products and built empires, and they have influence that stretches into the global space. They are eloquent and elegant; and while you have some sense, you are not like these women. You don't really fit in.

Standing there in my selfie pose, imposter syndrome was kicking in hard.

Even if you aren't familiar with the term "imposter syndrome," I bet you know the experience of feeling like a phony, as though at any moment you will be found out as a fraud. Compared to everyone else, you don't belong.

Imposter syndrome feeds right into the narratives of comparison, fear of insignificance, and approval addiction that we've been talking about. It reinforces the idea that says, "I am only loved for what I do. People will only accept me because of what I've accomplished. But what happens when they discover that I'm not up to their standard?"

Like comparison, imposter syndrome gains power when we focus on others instead of God. It causes us to make quick judgments about their worth compared to our own and to decide that we fall short. Then, preoccupied with the worry that they'll somehow discover how inadequate we are, we often downplay our God-given strengths and accomplishments; or we overemphasize them to overcompensate.

Naturally, these lies entirely miss the point.

The truth is that we all have something unique to bring to the group. We don't have to earn our place because God earned it for us through Jesus' sacrifice on the cross. We aren't being frauds when He plants us into a diverse group. We're ambassadors who share in His abundance.

"And God is able to bless you abundantly, so that in all things at all times, having all that you need, you will abound in every good work." 2 Cor 9:8

Imposter syndrome lies by saying that we lack something. But Paul contradicts this in the verse above by saying that we have *all that we need for* every good work.

In the very beginning of God's creation, He created ALL things and all things were created with unlimited potential to be fruitful and produce even more. All you ever needed, or could ever want, has been generously poured out in His beautiful creation from the beginning of time.

Here's the problem: The world we live in today runs into a tension between the truth of God's generosity and the myth of scarcity. Scarcity says that someone else's success is a threat to mine. Someone else's provision is a danger to me. Fear rises when we get drenched in these thinking patterns.

The truth is, there is room at the table for *all* of us. We don't have to prove that we belong or believe that what we need is on the verge of running out. Rather than compare ourselves to others, we rise when we *lift* others. When we can celebrate the success of another, we are living abundantly. When we can do this without the insecurity that comes from feeling like imposters who fall short compared to others, we're really living abundantly.

When you decide to contribute to this world with the giftings, the skills, the voice, and the contribution that is uniquely *you*, then you are living out 2 Cor 9:8, "And God is able to bless you abundantly, so that in all things at all times, having all that you need, you will abound in every good work."

God *is* able to bless you abundantly. You. Not just her or him or the mythical they that so often takes up residence in your head. You! He will provide you with more than enough of every kind of grace. There is sufficiency. There is no lack in God. He has all the grace you need.

"The truth is,
there is room
at the table for
all of us."

I didn't need a valet-worthy car or a Louis Vuitton bag. I didn't need strings of zeros in my income, or "global reach" for my influence. I had access to God's abundance and didn't have to earn or prove myself in any way.

Of course, I'm not suggesting that we don't need to work. Work, like abundance, is part of creation. In fact, I love to work. If anything, I want you to be passionate about what you do and the pursuit of your God-given purpose. But too often we work so that we can feel accepted and admired. And the moment we sense that we don't measure up, our inner voice calls us frauds for not being further along. I want to encourage you to stop wishing you were further along, believing that somehow you should be doing better like "them." Stay in your lane. Only look back to see how far you've come, and only look far enough ahead to remind you where you are going. As for the right and left, glance those directions to celebrate the ones beside you. But don't use their accomplishments to heap shame upon yourself. When they win... applaud. But stay in your lane.

Allow yourself to grow into where you're going. You might be taking a step into something new, like I was at that event of dreamers and movers. Don't define yourself or others by the limited space of scarcity. God is taking you somewhere. How wonderful to know that what you have is not all that God has. In His abundance, He still has more in store for you.

This may not result in all the same gifts and blessings that others receive or even all your dreams coming true right now. It may not equal crushing every goal on your list. But when you take another step closer to Jesus, with a settled heart and a mind that says "I already belong because I am His," you begin to feel His freedom. The magnitude of what you are doing or not doing is less important than the assurance of His plans for you.

So, back to the mirror in the luxurious bathroom in Laguna Niguel. My imposter syndrome moment had flared up, but it was fading as I clung to the truths we've just unpacked.

I stared square into the mirror, standing on marble floors suited for a queen. "That's me right there. I'm the one I'm looking at. It's time to focus on what's right in front of my face and stop consuming myself with everyone else. It's time to appreciate the work that God's put in my hands and the path He has faithfully led me on. It's time to strap on my reduced-priced, off-brand heels, put on my lipstick, hold my head up high and remember again who I belong to and where my inheritance comes from. Time to remember who provides every opportunity and enables the breath in my lungs. I am His pick, His chosen one. I am a daughter of the King. I belong here."

And with that, I decided. I decided I had a gift to bring to build God's Kingdom. I decided to own my worth. I decided to let go of doubt. I decided to use my gifts to create. I decided to serve humanity. I decided to live uncomfortably. I decided to increase my faith. I decided to collaborate and celebrate and end the game of comparison, competition, and imposter syndrome. And I decided to walk into rooms some might say I was not qualified to be in because I was a woman walking worthy of my calling.

> *I decided I had a gift to bring to build God's Kingdom.*

These choices are key for all of us. The decision to want what God wants for your life—to trust that it will fully satisfy—will increase your confidence no matter what room you're walking into, no matter who's there. And it will lead to a life that is much more fun! It will force you into new and uncomfortable things. It's the transition from known to unknown, normal to new, from status quo to elevation, maintenance to growth.

These decisions transition us from comparison to confidence. Transition is always challenging. There will be wrestling internally. You will need to contend for the truth as you roll into the Ritz Carlton and aren't the top, the smartest, or the most influential in the room. That fraudulent feeling that comes up in you can work for your good if you lean into what's happening. Listen to Jesus, do what He says, and decide not to allow all the lies to trigger all the old insecurities. That is not you anymore.

Decide that while you face internal opposition, *there is no external competition.* Falling into that trap will short-circuit your worth and diminish your dream. You're not an imposter. You're like me—a child of God created to do good works that He has prepared in advance for you to do. So, kill off all other options, keep deciding to follow with faith in your heart, and focus on Him.

Decide. Focus. Stay humble. And then receive His grace—His supernatural ability to do through you and for you what you cannot do for yourself. You have nothing to prove. Only something to give. So, grab your bag, put on your shoes, hop in whatever car you're rolling in and let's go to the Ritz.

12

YOUR TRUE IDENTITY

When our oldest daughter, Addison, was going into the fifth grade, we changed schools. The principal suggested that we prepare and share with her new classmates about Down syndrome and all the things they could expect when interacting with her. I knew in my gut it was the right thing to do. But first, we needed to talk to Addie. At this point, we had not even told our daughter about Down syndrome. It's just not the language that we used to define her. But the time had come to have the hard conversation. And so Marcus and I decided to call for a family meeting with the full Jones Tribe, party of six.

I don't think I've ever been more nervous about having a conversation in my life. I mapped it all out. I thought through all the contingencies. I blocked out an entire evening. I had an answer to every question. I had tissues ready for the weeping and gnashing of teeth. I braced myself for the torrent of emotion I was sure would come.

And so, we told them: "Kids, Mom and Dad love you so much. And we want you to know that Addison has Down syndrome."

There were two responses:

Addie's, "I DO? YES!! I have Down syndrome! Awesome!"

And the other kids, "Yeah, we kinda knew that. It's just Addie."

A bit surprised by their unflinching responses, I launched into my sober opening statement, but within two minutes, they all asked if they could go play. My huge issue was in fact a non-issue. These kids intrinsically knew that Addie's unique abilities and challenges were not connected to her value as a daughter of the King.

It wasn't a big deal. Addie wasn't her diagnosis. Addie was Addie— her gifts, talents, qualities, and yes, challenges, didn't limit her capability. I was the one bracing for the thunderclap of disappointment that never came. A medical diagnosis wasn't going to define what she could do or couldn't do. Her identity was already a settled issue, and it wasn't based on what she was capable of; it was based on *whose* she was.

The same is true for you and me.

Of course, it's one thing to know in principle that our identities are settled. But it's harder to accept in practice. Our whole lives are marked by identity formation. It's a process that's impacted by a variety of internal and external factors like society, family, loved ones, ethnicity, race, culture, location, opportunities, media, interests, appearance, self-expression and life experiences. Some of these things we choose. Some we are subject to. Some have been helpful, others hurtful. Some we desire and some we despise. Regardless of what has shaped you, identity is core to what causes us to think, believe, and often behave the way we do.

I know that one of the greatest challenges on my road to significance has been my ongoing struggle with identity. As you've read, it's a journey that has not been one-and-done for me but more like an onion whose layers keep peeling back through stages.

On this journey, I have become an overcomer. Unexpected and unwanted crises have become my friends because they've invited me to confront the many lies I've believed about identity. And then understand the Biblical truth that to gain my life, I must lose it.

I shared with you about the many years I told myself things like, "If I don't grind it out, I'm worthless," or "I'm all on my own—if I don't do it, then who will?" I was determined to matter and the only way that would ever happen was if I did exactly that: *make it all happen.*

Without success, I deemed myself unworthy. Without the external successes I considered significant, my value was diminished, and I just kept running after more. This kind of living is a trauma response. I was chasing lies, and the Enemy was using this hustle to keep me spinning.

Here's a question that helped me begin to break free from the spinning: *Who is defining you?*

When the story that you tell yourself is destructive, when it shuts you down and shuts you up, it's the Enemy of your soul, not God. You get to decide which story to listen to. Look to God's Word, to what He says. Replace destructive thinking with the truth by overwhelming dark thoughts with thoughts of the light.

"We can demolish every deceptive fantasy that opposes God and break through every arrogant attitude that is raised up in defiance of the true knowledge of God. We capture, like prisoners of war, every thought and insist that it bow in obedience to the Anointed One." 2 Corinthians 10:5 TPT

No matter your challenge, no matter your setback, no matter what you even believe about yourself, His words are truth. When your identity is in Christ you have nothing to prove, only something to give. True significance is not something to be attained—*it is a state of being.* It's who you are, and it is defined by our divine Creator.

"When your identity is in <u>Christ</u> you have nothing to <u>prove</u>, only something to <u>give</u>."

Some of you have had your identity stolen. And some, like me, have fallen into the wrong belief that your identity was something to be attained "out there." (Wherever *there* is.) The result is striving and then eventually shutting down because our efforts are never enough.

God, ever so graciously on the path of pain, reminded me clearly of what He says about us.

WE ARE CHOSEN AND COMPLETELY ACCEPTED

We all have wounds of rejection. Often, we base how well we are doing on the acceptance or approval of others. Instead, we should look first to God's approval. The rejection and longing for acceptance from others seasons absolutely EVERYTHING. Some of us are in a wrong career or in a bad relationship or hanging on to an old way of thinking because of the power of acceptance. God says, "I got you. Walk away and come with me."

WE ARE EXTREMELY VALUABLE

On my wedding day over twenty years ago, I received a gift during our ceremony. The pastor marrying us began to describe the union of two hearts coming together in unity through marriage. He talked of the incredible worth of two becoming one, and its immeasurable value. He then proceeded to pull out a necklace with a large heart-shaped gold pendant hanging from the center. It was unique and very pretty. And then he shared to whom it had belonged.

This was the necklace Jennifer Lopez had worn in the music video of one her biggest hits that year. He had tracked it down and found it in a Hollywood store that had relics from movie and music video sets. At that moment, the value of the necklace increased for me. It wasn't just the beauty of the jewelry that made it worth something. It was who had owned it. This belonged to J. Lo.

And you belong to God. Your worth is connected to being a child of the King, making you extremely valuable. If you never achieved another thing, you matter because of your identity as a child of God.

WE ARE LOVED

This is one of those statements that feels more complicated. I grew up my entire life singing the song, "Jesus loves me, this I know, for the Bible tells me so." It's a truth that should solidify into a sure foundation. But it's a profound statement that often takes a while to sink in.

For me, it happened one afternoon as I sat at a stoplight right off the freeway on the way to my house. This was a routine route, filled with the same sidewalks lining the streets with the same houses and same direction of traffic, everything as usual. As I stared out my window watching the neighbors walking and waiting for the light to turn green, a small, still voice inside said the words, "Jesus loves me."

This statement of faith that I knew and had said so many times sunk in on that day in a brand new way and has stayed with me since. I believe that this same experience can happen for you because I believe that Jesus loves you as He loves me.

WE ARE FORGIVEN

I know that God knows it all (and by "it," I mean my sin), and He's not surprised. He's never shocked. He is Yahweh Hesed, the God who forgives. He forgives *wholeheartedly*, and He has cast my sin into the sea of forgetfulness. I've been cleansed. I'm clean.

But it is me, it is we, who so often fall back into shame, in spite of His forgiveness. "If they really knew" are the words that bind us from truly being free. There have been offenses I have made when my heart is overwhelmed with, "I can't believe I did that." God does and **it's done**. Let it be done in you, too.

WE ARE FULLY CAPABLE

For far too long I set out to win and do big things because that's what I thought made me great. Sometimes I was first and often I wasn't, and my emotional well-being and confidence rode the wave of highs and lows, success or failure.

But capability isn't about my success or failure. This was a lesson I learned from Addie.

When Addie started high school, it was scary. Her school was the oldest in the city, gathered thousands of students from very diverse situations; and it was in a rough, urban environment. The contrast of needs for students with every language, ethnicity, neurodivergence, and socio-economic background was beautiful...and challenging.

Up to this point, Addie had continued to grow in her independence. Just like any other kid, we would drop her off at the front of the school. She had friends she would greet and a routine of putting her backpack up and grabbing her stuff. She found her way to her classes and, like many, enjoyed most of it. But this felt different. This was high school, and she would be learning everything again from scratch.

My heart panicked as I walked her to school, but with each step up the stairs I could hear her say, "I got this. You can do it. I can. I can." My tears flowed. I was blown away by the big person my little girl was becoming.

A few months into the school year we were due to meet with Addie's entire support team for an annual Individualized Education Plan (IEP). As a legal document that was binding and signed in ink, these meetings were always a little nerve-wracking. The decisions we'd make would determine a lot about the services and support Addie would receive.

Before her support team could fully project forward, they took a hard look at her current reality. They began to check boxes of a few of her "cans" but so many "can'ts" that Addie was not performing. Most of the boxes left unchecked were measured by the performance of typically developing kids, including reading level, ability to comprehend higher forms of mathematics, ability to construct a written paragraph in a certain time frame, and how many words she could type per minute.

Though I appreciated her team's candor and their jobs as educational instructors to help Addie continue to make progress and grow with higher level learning, I finally had to speak up. Our goals for Addie have never been a Harvard Law Degree. Our goals have always been that she connect in the community, have confidence to communicate, and have meaningful relationships. We desire her to build her strength of independence by trying new things. And most importantly, our heart for Addie is that she discover her God-given gifts that ultimately lead to purpose-filled work for her as an adult.

And so I opened my mouth with a bit of fear and trembling, and I said to a round table of fifteen highly-educated professionals:

"You are missing it. You are limiting her potential and her worth because you are missing who she is by only looking at what she can or can't do. It is in the becoming that she will soar and do great things. Do you understand the bravery being cultivated in this process? Do you value the tenacity in each step she is taking? Do you realize the strength of character required to show up with her limited abilities? That is what creates her impact. That is what causes her to rise head and shoulders above the others. This is what will enable her to thrive in a culture and world where she swims upstream. This is the stuff that will help Addie survive well beyond the public school classroom."

And that is also true of me and you! Our becoming is far more valuable than our doing. The hard part of becoming is that it is often forged through difficulty; suffering is the unwelcome catalyst. In so many ways, my doing and "checking the boxes of transactional actions" like Addie's evaluation, was limiting my ability to truly fulfill my purpose. This is also true for you. It can be easy to focus solely on a task list and never allow your life to go deeper or be seen beyond the surface.

You are significant. Not for what you've done or haven't done, where you've been or where you are going. Simply because you are *you*. And wherever you find yourself TODAY is part of the path that is enabling you to live out the dream, the story, and the God-ordained plan God has promised for you.

Enough with the self-bullying, downplaying, demeaning talk, and shaming yourself. Start today. Right where you are—it's not too late; you haven't missed out. Stop looking back. Just put one foot in front of the other and keep on stepping toward the truth, which is that our identity is and must be found in Christ alone.

> *Our becoming is far more valuable than our doing.*

He wants us to know who and *whose* we are. We're cherished, chosen, and empowered people of God, handcrafted for an eternal purpose. Our value doesn't increase when we reach our goals, get promoted, or publish a best-selling book. Nor does it decrease when we're laid off or encounter rejections.

Knowing this, and anchoring our hearts in grace, frees us from the idol of success and enables us to become all we were meant to be.

Section 3

TRUE
CALLING

13

WHOLEHEARTED YES (NO STRINGS ATTACHED)

The initial blindside of my husband's exit from the mega church was rough. It was the path we thought was our forever future. The shock of being forced to resign felt like death. It was an incredible loss. A dream died.

Amid this grief, a plan was forming. *I wasn't sure that I liked it.* But a direction was rising to the surface. My husband was burdened to do something radical for Christ in the city's center, and he believed that the mission would require us to start a church right in the heart. I was in alignment with this decision, even though the thought of failure had me afraid.

Statistically speaking, most church plants do fail, and urban church plants fail at an even faster rate, often struggling even to launch. There are a lot of reasons behind these realities, and we talked about all of them as we were jumping off this cliff. In spite of the head winds, we forged ahead, eyes wide open in radical obedience to Christ.

My new business opportunity as a health coach was less scary, but it annoyed me. I was angry at God and very irritated by His ways. As if the loss of our job, community, kids' security, and financial stability wasn't enough, we were now doing the gut-wrenching work of church planting in the city's trenches. And on top of all this, I had to provide money through a vehicle I'd never heard of and didn't even want.

It seemed so unfair of God to ask so much of me.

This wasn't my first time with these kinds of feelings. It wasn't the first time I'd asked, "God, why are you doing this to me?" When Addie was born, I wrestled intensely with my faith. The reality of my firstborn daughter's diagnosis of Down syndrome leveled me with doubt. Doubt in me. Doubt in her future. Doubt in God and distrust in humanity. I was scared, caught unaware, and it broke my heart wide open.

Of course, God came through in that situation. Addie's arrival turned my world upside down and changed everything. A small, seven-pound bundle of joy with an extra twenty-first chromosome transformed me significantly. Her life, her diagnosis, and her story reprioritized everything. She is the best gift I never knew I wanted.

My experience with Addie reminded me that sometimes, God takes you on a journey you never knew you needed to give you everything you ever wanted. Addie had taught me many years ago the power of trusting in God's plan. Because of her, I could say YES. It was seeing the miraculous lived out through her story that enabled me to keep my faith and empowered my next step toward my calling.

Over the years, I've had to dig deep and cling to hope. I've often wanted to avoid the pain and difficulty. But when I've embraced the challenges and contended through obstacles, I've received the gift of becoming.

And now I was faced with another chance. This was my chance to replace "But I DON'T WANT TO!" with "God, now what?"

What falls into the big, fat, firm, "I don't want to" category for you? Throughout my life, there have been a few of these poignant moments. I can almost hear the conversations I've had with God over the years:

I don't want to have a child with Down syndrome, God.

I don't want to be a health coach.

I don't want to move my kids and put them in another school, Lord. And an inner city one at that.

It's a hard NO, God! I don't want to.

At the heart of all this push-back is always the fear of the unknown. It comes with an assumption that what's unknown must inevitably be painful. And let's be honest, most of us will do anything to avoid discomfort. But often going through the unknown is the only way to go from resisting in fear to embracing in faith. There is no way around it; there is only through.

The process of growing through a hardship—of accepting the path of "I don't want to" (which has sometimes ended exactly as I expected)—is the only way to move from resistance to trust, from anxiety to peace. We have hope for the future and that propels us forward. But it is the arms clinging tightly hugged around faith that grounds us in calm.

In Numbers 13, Moses sends out twelve spies into the land of Canaan—the Promised Land. This was the land God was giving as a birthright to His people. But instead of entering in trust, the spies retreated in anxiety. This was the intelligence report they brought back to Moses:

> *"We entered the land you sent us to explore, and it is indeed a bountiful country—a land flowing with milk and honey. Here is the kind of fruit it produces. But the people living there are*

powerful, and their towns are large and fortified. We even saw giants there... But Caleb tried to quiet the people as they stood before Moses. 'Let's go at once to take the land,' he said. 'We can certainly conquer it!' But the other men who had explored the land with him disagreed. 'We can't go up against them! They are stronger than we are!'" Numbers 13:27-31 NLT

They didn't want to. They were afraid, uncertain, inconvenienced, and insecure. Despite all the fruit and hopeful prospects for the future in this fertile land, what they lacked was faith.

We all have these moments, don't we? We all walk through the wilderness at times saying, "But I don't want to."

But it's when we say "yes," owning our feelings without letting them own us, and accept God's invitation to faith that we enter into God's fruitful process of growth and transformation. It's embracing God's opportunity to mature, develop, and transform us. These moments ready us for the very things we desire most. Our yes to the "I don't want to" in our life moves us out of self-reliance and into dependence on Christ. And this is where the magic happens. This is how the more abundant life is received.

We all want the *daring yes* to be *glam*, but a daring yes actually requires *grit*. Each next "yes" step draws us closer to our promised purpose in Christ. Our part is *faith* to believe in what we cannot see.

God has made the promise. Our job is to trust in His faithfulness. Those who shrink back in skepticism never see the Promised Land. But those who follow in faith will live in the blessing.

Numbers 32:11-12 tell the rest of the story:

"Of all those I rescued from Egypt, no one who is twenty years old or older will ever see the land I swore to give to Abraham,

Isaac, and Jacob, for they have not obeyed me wholeheartedly.
The only exceptions are Caleb son of Jephunneh the Kenizzite
and Joshua son of Nun, for they have wholeheartedly
followed the LORD."

A wholehearted yes is entirely and sincerely devoted, no matter what. The answer is obedience. Obedience makes the determination to never give up—to outlast the Enemy and win the victory. And along the journey, the Lord often spends time transforming us before He transforms our circumstances.

Back to my predicament: I knew from my experience with Addie that saying "yes" was the best path. So, I dove in. I was obedient. We followed the Lord with reckless abandon in every area of our life. It felt right. I was giving Jesus all that I could, and it felt good. It was a privilege to do so in every regard.

My yes was fruitful. But there was one small shadow tainting that yes that God had to uncover for me to find the complete freedom He wanted for me. That shadow was the condition I was putting on my yes without even knowing it.

You see, I assumed that my wholehearted surrender and pursuit of His will would fulfill our vision. Deep down, I counted on everything aligning; I imagined our story would be about how everything worked out just as we imagined in Jesus' name and for His glory.

Perhaps you've made this assumption as well. It goes like this: *I'm obedient. I do the right things, so God will have everything work out, right? Why wouldn't He? He's asked, I've answered. I can see it. He can do it. It's the perfect match. Let's go.*

These thoughts are natural, normal, and common. But they also point to something that isn't aligned with God's design. I call it "having

"Obedience makes the determination to never give up— to outlast the Enemy and win the victory."

a transactional attitude with God." And you won't find it in His playbook for you.

A transactional attitude assumes that if I do A, then God will have to do B.

If I wholeheartedly plant a church for God's glory, then God will surely help it grow and succeed. If I pour my heart into my first book, using it to serve Him and share His story, then God will pave a way for it to be published and gain influence. If I'm out on a limb of faith, starting a new business that I never imagined I'd be doing, then God will certainly use it as a way to fuel the work I really want to do, right?

You get the idea.

If we're honest, most of us want our destiny on demand. We want all of God's promises to not only be yes and amen. We want them yes, amen, now, and precisely the way we imagined.

> *If we're honest, most of us want our destiny on demand.*

And then when it turns out... well ...not on our terms, it can be a bitter pill to swallow. These letdowns are what the Enemy uses to discourage us—to entice us to begin saying *No* instead of *Yes*. We grow skeptical, get cynical, and become guarded.

But what if God knows our deepest desires even better than we do? What if the outcomes He has in store for us are unexpected surprises?

Think about it: If God always met your expectations per "the transaction," He would never have the opportunity to *exceed* them. We hold ridiculously tight, with a white knuckle-fisted grip, to what we think we are entitled to in this life. So when something doesn't go our way, when we lose control, and the outcomes we desire keep slipping through our fingers, we are faced with a choice. Do we surrender our transactional attitude; or do we hustle harder, hold on tight, and keep running and gunning like it's all on us?

That second plan may work out (temporarily), but then you would give yourself all the credit and believe that somehow you are in control. And if it is *you* that determines all your success, then it is also you who is responsible for all your failures. Now you're on both sides of the transaction, carrying all the liability.

I do not want that level of responsibility over my life or any others. I just can't deliver.

The reality of God's plans for you and me are too big for us to achieve on our own. In the moment, it can seem like He's not delivering on His part of the bargain, but we don't see all that He sees. We can't comprehend all that He knows. When our challenges loom the largest is when God shows us just how big He is.

May your heart see the hope of God's plan for you. May you be overcome by His goodness that's working on your behalf as you step into the next unknown. And may the truth of His promises overwhelm your heart and enable you to turn from your hard NO into a daring YES!

14

ODE TO OBEDIENCE

In my early twenties, I traveled the globe on a mission to see the world changed for the good. I spoke in other countries and led large events in urban schools. I facilitated camps for students and was "changing the world." And then?

Then I became a hair salon receptionist.

I sat in a salon for two years, greeting people and chatting it up with stylists from behind a receptionist's desk. During that time, hidden behind a phone and facial product displays, God led me to the next step. I didn't know it then, but that season of stillness was a moment God was doing something extraordinary.

That was the season I became a wife and embarked on the adventure of marriage. That was the season I learned new and challenging things. God drew me (and grew me) out of the spotlight. My path led me to sit in a front desk chair of obscurity. And it was there in that noisy salon where pride was crucified in me. It was the place God hid me in plain sight and revealed more of Himself to me.

In the years that followed, I would have four kids. I spent much of my time at home, wiping and cleaning and cooking and crying on wash, rinse, and repeat. It was not a glamorous season. It was not filled with lights, cameras, or action. In fact, most days, it was a win if I got a good shower. I didn't feel like I accomplished much, and when people asked what I was doing, my timid response was, "I'm just a mom."

I remember a pastor once called me out on that phrase. He heard the contempt in the word "just" and challenged my thinking. How could the role of raising four humans that God created be "just" anything? That's what I was saying with "just" a mom. I minimized the incredible calling it is to hold the hearts of four tiny humans. I demeaned my position of incredible influence among the most precious gifts I had been given. I didn't see the bigness in my momming littles.

I craved greatness. My appetite to achieve, accomplish, do, and perform was insatiable. For a large part of my life, I had little awareness that character and internal growth were something to be valued. Mostly, I measured growth by outward indicators. I took the bull by the horns when those measurements weren't clicking. I called it *determination*, but it was also ego. Pride drove my actions. And sometimes at great cost. I was often exhausted, discouraged, and burnt out.

My drive and hustle so often came from a place of needing someone else's approval. It came from a longing for the crowd's applause. During seasons when God assigned me to "sit in the chair of obscurity," I wrestled with feeling unsatisfied. Everything just seemed to fall flat. Even the achievements I did accomplish fell short, pushing me toward a new milestone and into a striving that kept me spinning.

Yet again, I was measuring my worth based on what the world considered success. Staying home with my babies pinched my ego. It went against my pride and all my perceived ability. *Was it not enough in that season to care for these precious gifts, birthed in the image of Christ?*

Yes, it was mundane, but God met me amidst the tedium and let me know that my work was not my worth. I could wish that I was in a bigger or better place. But I heard the gentle whisper of the Lord say, "Here. Invest *here*. Everything else you do will be out of the abundance of this gift."

This simple admonition brought me peace. A word from God always will. The surrender required to walk in His calling might bring discomfort, but His grace will cover you. It did for me. And in surrender, you will gain the ability to be still.

In my season of surrender, I stopped. I stopped trying so hard to do so many things. I focused my intention inside my four walls. And for almost a decade, that was it.

During that time, a truth was sown into my heart: obedience to God's leading is always *the most trustworthy place you can be.*

I have fallen more in love with God through this refining process. It has sometimes been painful to feel hidden. The seasons when I felt unseen have been hard. But my sense of loss created a desperation for more of God that said, "Your will be done." I discovered the key to success—the secret of my significance—would depend on my obedience to God.

Health coaching was a big part of this journey. There were moments when I was embarrassed to admit what I did for a living. Coaching was never a dream for me. It wasn't the title or position I ever wanted to pursue. I often asked God, "Why? Why so obscure? Why so far outside the way I thought things were supposed to be? Why so often hidden and misunderstood?"

At one point, a "spiritual authority" accused me of forsaking my "true calling" because I had decided to move from ministry to health coaching. This not only took any wind out of my sails, but it convinced me I had really missed the boat. I was sometimes embarrassed and

"Obedience to God's leading is always the most trustworthy place you can be."

ashamed of my path. This shame revealed that my highest goal was to preserve the image I had tried to hustle for myself. But when this realization finally dawned on me, I was drawn into surrender—a vulnerability to hide in God—to exchange my rawness and weakness for His strength. In that process, I trained myself to keep my eyes fixed on Him and my identity rooted in Him.

This was the path of obedience. These were the moments that I learned what obedience really looks like. Jenny Donnelly says it best in her book, *Still: 7 Ways to Find Calm in the Chaos.*

> *"This is where I see people trip into the biggest pothole on their way toward a fruitful life in God. When the Gardener gives you instructions, it's in your best interest to obey, not because God is going to be outraged with you if you don't but because he has more for you. The 'more' is the product of obedience. He is trying to grow some big fat fruit on your branches."*[3]

Obedience will bring you rest. Disobedience produces anxiety. God does not want to dominate harshly but rather guide you with His goodness. He is brightness and light—there is no darkness in Him. He leads with faithfulness and strength. His plan is always better than we expect. Surrendering to God's leadership brings about a realization: when I listen to Jesus and do what He says, I operate in my superpower: obedience.

A couple of years ago, I was traveling for work in another state. I received a direct message on Instagram from someone I did not know.

"You are in my town. Can you come to my work? I have a baby with Down syndrome. I'm hurting so badly, and nobody knows."

---

[3] *Donnelly, Jenny L.* Still: 7 Ways to Find Calm in the Chaos. *Revell, a Division of Baker Publishing Group, 2020.*

At that moment, I heard the whisper of God say, "Go!"

"Yes!" I replied. "What's your address? I'll be there tomorrow at 11 am."

I had no idea if who I was about to visit was real. Was this a sham? Was I about to be robbed and left for dead in some dark alley? (See how doubt and fear always like to show up as uninvited and often irrational guests to your faith party?) But amidst these questions, I heard the whisper again, "Go!" Many years of serving Jesus have taught me to love listening to Him and doing what He says. *Obedience.*

I arrived not knowing what to expect. I left an hour later personally and radically transformed. The encounter I had with this precious mom was holy. It was an honest heart desperate to be held, and I was honored to do so. In this situation, I, a stranger who understood the depths of what it meant to hold the unexpected diagnosis of Down Syndrome, was exactly what her soul needed.

The reality of this encounter was beyond what I could even imagine orchestrating. It was divine. Me, on my way out of Texas going back to California, receives an Instagram message from an acquaintance of an acquaintance, with only hours to spare before my flight leaves; and we are able to connect on one of the deepest levels I have ever experienced with another human. All that in just sixty minutes. I was blown away at the power of the Holy Spirit to change a life and fill a heart when I'm simply willing to follow His gentle voice and obey His command.

I'll never forget a few weeks later, she texted me. She wanted to know more about who I was and what I did. It wasn't so much about my job title or my actual daily grind. She asked what I was called to and why I thought our interaction was impactful and created such lasting effects.

Answering was difficult, but I resisted the cliché to say, "It wasn't me; it was God." Quickly, though, the answer occurred to me: *Obedience.* I'm called to obedience. I have been faithful in pain. Now obedience has become my joy.

Building a bridge of love doesn't require a badge or fancy position. What my new-found friend encountered that day wasn't because of a job title. The ingredients were simple, but the result was profound: my obedience, folded in with her honesty, resulted in a holy interaction.

Obedience is our superpower.

I'm happy I didn't compartmentalize my life that day. I'm glad I didn't neglect the opportunity to obey by brushing off her cry for help. "No, I'm sorry, I can't come to meet you. I'm here for my health coach business. This is #bosslady week, not a parenting seminar."

As women, we often celebrate (and commiserate about) the reality that we wear many hats. However, I've heard it said, "Hats are for hiding; you wear a crown."

When we stop living in rigid, controlled compartments and start seeing our lives as beautiful gardens, we become more open to the adventure of obedience. God breaks down the walls between our compartments and leads us into holy moments. Just because something doesn't look the way you expect doesn't mean it's not an invitation to step into your superpower.

> *Obedience is our superpower.*

Yes, there will be times when God leads you through the desert. There will be delayed promises and death to what you think you deserve. During these times, obedience is difficult. It requires us boldly professing that God is good even when things seem bad. Obedience means activating our faith with the audacious trust that God will deliver in time. His goodness chases us. By relying on Him through obedience, He calls us to a higher place so that we will bear good fruit.

Obedience has been required to create the life God has called me to, and it demands incredible intention. The Enemy of your soul will attack the person you are to become. That man or woman is imbued with the hope of tomorrow.

You have a destiny—a future—filled with promises backed by the Sovereign God Himself. The Enemy will do everything he can to see that thwarted. But he is a defeated foe. Make the obedience shift for the you that is under construction—the person who is just ahead. The you who has embraced the hard things, still struggles in the dark days yet confidently rests in the promise of your Father who says, "I will complete the work I have started."

You have a powerful destiny in Christ—a future full of promises held under complete warranty from your Heavenly Father. His loving kindness toward you never flinches or fails. He is shaping something spectacular in you—something significant. The work is already underway. And the great news is God always finishes what He starts.

15

OBEDIENCE LOOKS LIKE FRIENDSHIP

I was nineteen years old when I started in ministry. I went away to Arizona to be part of a radical group of zealous young Christians. We committed our lives for one year to be discipled and fully know God. Our passion was to travel to the largest cities in America and abroad to spread His love and make Him known. It was when I first felt the tug to live my life with radical abandon: to fulfill the call of God.

"Here I am, Lord, send me," was often my cry. It was then that I committed to a life of obedience no matter the cost. But over time, I found myself wondering *who* I was obeying. I had operated under the impression that it was God, but the voice barking inside my head often sounded more like a drill sergeant than a Deliverer. This voice bullied me, demanding that I sacrifice joy and peace for "the cause." I felt like it was my duty to ensure that all of the city came to Christ. It's all on YOU, Jen. I hung on to Luke 11:9-10:

*"So I say to you: Ask, and it will be given to you; seek, and
you will find; knock, and the door will be opened to you.
For everyone who asks receives; the one who seeks finds;
and to the one who knocks, the door will be opened."*

I kept asking, kept hoping, and kept praying. The unanswered questions, and the unmet wants, made me worry that, even after the next step of obedience, another ball would inevitably drop.

*Am I really on track? Am I doing what you want, God? Because it seems like
the steps I am taking aren't pulling things together the way I'd hoped; instead,
it's as though it's all falling apart.*

My fears of yet another blindside were deeply connected to my picture of God. What do *you* think about when you think about God? What's the picture in your head?

Scripture often describes Him as a father. Do you see Him this way? As a parent myself, it's hard to imagine being aloof or non-responsive to my kids. Yet this is sometimes how I feel about God when I am waiting longer than I think I should.

No matter if your circumstances cause you to paint a picture of God as a task master, domineering force or a cosmic killjoy, we must look to the words of the Scripture which accurately define the true character and personhood of God. In one of my harder days, I was comforted by another description of God: *Philos,* meaning friend.

*"This is My commandment, that you love one another, just as
I have loved you. Greater love has no one than this, that one
lay down his life for his friends. You are My friends if you
do what I command you. No longer do I call you slaves, for
the slave does not know what his master is doing; but I have
called you friends, for all things that I have heard from My
Father I have made known to you. You did not choose Me but*

*I chose you, and appointed you that you would go and bear
fruit, and that your fruit would remain, so that whatever
you ask of the Father in My name He may give to you. This I
command you, that you love one another." John 15:12-17*

We see in this passage that Jesus calls us friends. Could it be that likewise, we can call Him friend?

It's important to point out that this Scripture ties our friendship to our obedience. Jesus wants us all in. Not because we are His slaves. Not because He wants to boss us around like some cosmic control freak, high in the sky, waving His list of demands, but because we are friends.

We learn in this passage that true friends share secrets; they share intimate details with one another. We see that we are to consider our friends as more important than ourselves, willing to lay down our own lives to help them. We see that friends are to love one another. We learn that true friends believe in one another and that God often sees more in us than we believe for in Him. But that is the level of intimacy Christ is calling us to.

And if the cost is obedience, the reward is rich.

According to John 15, when Jesus told the disciples that they were His friends, He gave them a mission. He was saying, "You are the Bridegroom's friends. You are the friends who will serve the world on my behalf." Being a friend of Jesus is about living His love out loud.

When we know God as a friend, we know He is *always* our friend. His friendship with us is tied to His commitment to us, as we have committed to Him. Our friendship with God is not based on our perfection; it's rooted in our *connection*.

My best friend and I have a lot in common which cultivates a ton of fun. But what binds us tightly is the deep appreciation and admiration for our differences. It is the honor of one another despite all the things

"Our friendship with God is not based on our perfection; it's rooted in our connection."

that make us different. It is the hope for the good of the other, the celebration and elevation of each other regardless of the situation or circumstance. Because what makes her my best friend is who she is on the deeper level of personhood. It's a soul-to-soul thing.

That's what God is looking for with you: a soul-to-soul thing. A deep, personal relationship that shapes you and strengthens you and sets your feet securely on a life of significance. The investment is your obedience, but the reward is incalculable.

A true friend is someone who connects with you deeply. You can empathize with the other and often meet their needs without them saying anything. When that friend needs a word, you are free to give it. I don't have to ask my best friend to pray for me—she just does. When I do ask her to hop on a call because I need to talk, I never worry that she won't. When I'm in need, I never doubt she will do all she can to support me. And often, a timely word I need from God is delivered through my friend.

She is human, and of course, like me, limited. But God is not. How much more will God, our Friend and Counselor, be there for us? How much more is He rooting for us? He is not against you. He's your biggest fan. He will never harm you, never turn on you. He has promised to be with you to the end. And He wants you to bear fruit that lasts.

Knowing this truth and believing God is good did sometimes cause me to question why He would allow some things to happen and not others. For instance, with the church plant, there was so much confirmation along the way about our actions. He had provided financially beyond what I expected. He had given our faith community a home. There was an impact in our city, and the dream was unwavering; it hung on our wall. So why wouldn't God want it to come to pass? It was all so good. But in times of challenge, it was hard to see.

Oftentimes we want God to do good work *through* us but overlook the very thing that will cause the good work *in* us. God loves big dreams, but He loves us even more.

I had set out to restore the city. God had an agenda to restore *me* along the way. And so it is with you. God invites you to trust Him with your whole heart and no longer put your faith in the wrong things: your strengths, your experiences, your intellect. We are always in a position of choice. Will we hold back, afraid to fully let go of control? Or will we consider the facts about who God is and let the truth sink in: *He's not mean. He's your friend.*

> *God loves big dreams, but He loves us even more.*

As a friend, His kindness is drawing us out of dependence on our limited abilities, so we can find peace in relying on Him. Obedience that finds its rest in friendship with God.

Remember, it's a soul-to-soul thing. A deep, personal relationship that shapes you and strengthens you and sets your feet securely on a life of significance. And that friendship with God is never based on your perfection. It's rooted in your *connection*—connection to a faithful God who has gone to inexpressible lengths to call you friend.

16

OBEDIENCE LOOKS LIKE GOING AGAINST THE GRAIN

I'm not a rebel. I'm a dreamer and a doer. I don't take no for an answer most of the time. I like to persist and think outside of the box.

But I am a rule follower, a best-practices kind of girl. Tell me what works, and I'll make it happen. Give me a system to succeed, and I'll climb to the top. Building a business and becoming a health coach played to these strengths. Until obedience required me to go against the grain.

I was still receiving pushback about my new business from people in my church ministry space. Some circles of church leadership were big fans of bi-vocational service, and just as many said it would be the cause of our failure. A few admired my capacity to carry my business and ministry, but just as many considered me a sellout.

These voices were tormenting; and of course, they amplified the most prominent voice inside my head. But I persisted. Obedience was already challenging me to break molds and go against the noise in ministry. It was about to challenge me again in business.

When I joined forces with others in the health coach community, I immediately recognized that my "why" was different. I stood apart. Most had started their businesses to create something primary: primary relationships, primary purpose, primary passion, and primary income. But for me, business was secondary. I already had community, a purpose, and a passion for ministry. I just needed income to provide for some financial basics and enable the dream we had already set our hands to do.

> *I was going against the grain, and it worked until it didn't.*

Another common denominator among my new colleagues I didn't share was the trend of managing the business together as a couple. In fact, the most successful in the field were couples who had joined forces to grow their businesses together with their spouse. In contrast, I was it. Marcus had his hands full with the work of the church. He was in full support and aligned with the company values, but he was not committing to being a health coach.

I was going against the grain, and it worked until it didn't.

A few years into my business, I hit a lid with my growth. Until then, I had found rapid success as a trailblazer hitting top ranks, independently as a female without her husband's help. But when growth started slowing, outside experts began to diagnose what might be capping my growth. The diagnosis was that my solo status was holding me back. If I wanted to see another wave of momentum, my husband would need to join me.

Now don't get all upset; the intent was not sexist. It's just what had worked for so many. But instead of considering this descriptive, some made it prescriptive and decided this was the only way to win.

And so I found myself again challenged to the obedience that goes against the grain. Obedience for our home was for me to remain solo on this path and for Marcus to stay focused on his. Obedience did not equal easy, and it required sacrifice. I didn't always scale as fast as others in the company. My growth timeline was faster than some but not nearly as rapid as others.

Having dual drivers—ministry and health coaching—also divided my time. I was faced with hard decisions that forced me to choose between things that were *all* priorities. Sometimes they were simple, like skipping a Sunday service to be present at a business event. But other times, they were challenging and filled my heart with conflict.

For instance, our company hosted a leadership retreat in the mountains each year for the highest-ranking leaders. These were my colleagues and had become my dearest friends. The learnings we gained at this event were often catalytic to our growth in the year to come. It always occurred in the fall (last quarter) and was crucial for me to get my head straight for the coming year and first-quarter growth. We would also receive important information and gather in collaboration, which is one of my favorite parts of my business.

It was a weekend that had proven essential to success in the past, and I had never missed it. The value of this event was essential to me and was also critical to my leadership and ongoing success. So when my two oldest daughters' homecoming was scheduled on the exact same weekend, my heart began to panic. I quickly raced to find solutions, refusing to accept that I would have to miss out on either event. I scanned airlines for arrival and departure times, determined to make them work out.

How can I be in two places at once? How can I do what seems required for my
business and be present for this rare moment in my growing teenage girls' lives?

I know we love to believe that we can have it all, but I don't buy into
the enticing slogan that all is possible. Not all at once, anyway. I had to
choose between my business and my babies at this event. There was
no other way to spin the details—a choice would have to be made. And
while I could not be in two places simultaneously, I could go against
the grain and think outside the box.

I decided to leave the leadership retreat early. I flew to Utah and
attended the first forty hours of the six-day event. I left before the
morning of homecoming and got home in time to see the girls get ready
and be part of the festivities and photos before the dance. I decided
that, for this mom, work was important, but my kids were essential. It's
a decision that only works for some, and if you pointed to the rate of
growth in my business compared to others, it did slow me down.

I was mostly okay with these trade-offs, knowing that obedience
almost always required some sacrifice and trusting that God would fill
the gaps in His own way. But I was also learning that going against the
grain didn't automatically mean living an "either/or" life. I didn't have
to be either a ministry leader or a businesswoman.

A conversation that put this lesson into perspective happened on
a flight home from a business trip. I was rushing back to make it to
Sunday church services on time, and I had my oldest daughter, Addie,
with me.

Now, it's a sure thing, when you go anywhere with Addie, that you
will make friends. Whether it's in the line at Starbucks or at the pool
on vacation, if Addie is there, you'll walk away with an introduction,
a few fun facts, and a new connection on social media. This flight
home was the same. Addie and I were in the same row but separated
by the aisle. In the middle seat next to my daughter was a lovely,

middle-aged woman who smiled kindly and said "Hi" to Addie as she sat. That's all it took. The conversation and questions began.

After they had chatted for a while and the drinks and peanuts were being served, Addie felt it was time she introduced me. "Mom, this is Kelly. Kelly, this is my mom, Jen." This is the standard introduction Addie always gives. If there were more people and the rest of the family, she would have gone around the horn, ensuring every individual was seen. "Hi Kelly, it's nice to meet you."

And thus, the conversation that shifted my thinking about my obedience began.

Like most conversation starting points, the "occupation" question would come up. As the conversation continued with Kelly, I knew, at some point, it was inevitable. We went back and forth about parenting and family and what it looked like as we raised four kids. Sure enough, next came, "So Jen, what do you do for a living?"

It might sound strange, but the question made me uncomfortable because I still felt like my significance was riding on my answer. Kelly had already professed her faith to me. We talked a little about raising kids and going to church. But the truth is, I was traveling home from a business event to get to my church to lead the service on time. So what did I do for a living? I wasn't even sure how to summarize that for myself.

This stranger sitting next to Addie felt like she could be a friend, so I processed my unfiltered response out loud. "I'm not really sure how to answer that question," I replied.

And then, into a valiant plunge of oversharing, I blurted out, "I started a business that often feels missional. My intent from the beginning was to earn income because my husband and I are also pastors, and we recently started a church. I'm a pastor and a business leader, and they are mutually beneficial and align with my values. I can't fully explain how they work together because it's new for me too. So as awkward as I sound describing it out loud, internally, it feels even more so this way."

Her response to me brought incredible delight. In fact, it lifted a burden I'd been carrying for a couple years as pastor's wife and health coach.

"This is what my business model calls *living in the 'and'*," Kelly said.

This one word, "and", had me leaning in to learn more. She worked for a faith-based product sales company that earned income and engaged in the community. Its primary mission was to build one another up in faith and business.

> *I could be a health coach, a businesswoman, and a minister of God's word.*

Living in the "and" sounds so simple as I type these words, but it was so profound at that moment. I didn't have to compartmentalize as though I lived two separate lives. Obedience didn't require me to choose who I would be on Monday and change my approach on Wednesday. I didn't have to decide which was more essential and parse out my efforts, like picking favorites and leaving the rest with the crumbs. It was not a life of "or"; it was the life of "and". I could be a health coach, a businesswoman, *and* a minister of God's word.

This is the true integration we all long for—that all parts of our lives will become one. Obedience doesn't mean a life of always sacrificing one important thing for the other. When God leads us into obedience, all good things are mutually beneficial because He's ordering our lives and priorities.

This moment, this short fly through the sky, lifted the lid on my leadership and sent me soaring forward with a new lease on the life I was leading. It was life in the "and." It was a life that I hoped was possible but was a little afraid that I was wrongfully sacrificing one for the other. Or even that I wasn't being true to God or myself.

It wasn't about serving two masters. It was more about could the one I was serving enable me to live out my calling in two different vehicles, with multiple passions, at the same time? Perhaps I had seen others mishandle their family, and their business, and their ministry; and the cost was greater than I was ready to pay.

I was learning that while some have mishandled the things placed in their hands, that didn't mean it was impossible for me to create a healthy family and a fruitful ministry. My eyes were opened not to "or," but to "and".

I could be a present mom, a minister, and a successful businesswoman. It might be a little against the grain. But that was the road I was on. As you read on, I hope you will discover that this "life in the and" could be yours, too. This is divinely different. Not for the sake of juggling lots of things as some sort of badge of honor, but for the path of obedience to Christ. To hear His voice and respond in a way that might lead you on new and different paths and enrich you in more ways than you can possibly imagine.

17

OBEDIENCE SOMETIMES LOOKS LIKE FAILURE

Part of my healthy habit routine is physical movement. I've done this for years. As a health coach, it's vital to my personal health optimization and one of the habits I guide others to implement. Exercise has become a strategy for me to maintain energy and a higher level of mental and emotional health. Sometimes a few miles pounding the pavement is as good as an hour in my therapist's office.

In the immediate aftermath of our decision to resign from our church plant, before anyone had been informed yet, I went to one of my Orange Theory Fitness classes. The class was intense, and my body's stress made it even more intense. In the final moments of the workout, I felt a physical release that felt like exhilaration.

As I left the gym and headed to my car, I received a text from Doug, a friend and business mentor. He was checking in, as he frequently did. We were colleagues, and he was somewhat aware of our decision-making process. Up to this point, I had not spoken the words, "We are leaving the church," out loud, but I found myself responding in a text that Marcus and I were moving on from our beloved church plant. Immediately tears flowed down my cheeks, and I picked up my pace to get into my car. I could sense ugly crying coming on.

Saying it out loud, even in an audio message, made the reality much more powerful. Walking away was causing me a mental, emotional, and physical need to release a part of myself.

This was the end of an era. For my entire adult life, the only positions I'd ever held or income I'd ever earned came from a local church. Likewise, for almost twenty years, I'd held the title of "pastor's wife," and it had become an identity. I liked it. Somedays, I even loved it. I often wore it like a badge of honor and wanted to be known for it. I mean, *I hashtagged it.*

So as the "pastor's wife" chapter closed, I feared losing a piece of myself. The stark reality is that I was, and it hurt. My obedience was creating an unexpected crisis and what felt like confusion. As confident as I was in my walk with Christ, for as often as I helped others learn to hear His voice, these events unfolding in my life were painful. I questioned why it didn't feel better than this?

I took a day and went away to process, searching for the source of what was creating conflict for me. I never did things like this—it was virtually impossible with four kids—but I needed to navigate the overwhelming confusion I felt. I wanted to hear from God about what He expected of me in what felt like a losing battle.

As I prayed, it became clear that I didn't have much left and that laying down my sword for a bit was okay. Even the noblest knight sometimes must take a knee. Surrender doesn't mean never fighting again; it doesn't mean you've lost the war. Surrender means that this particular fight is not yours to win.

This realization was both scary and exhausting. I had to hash it out with my Creator, who has never lost a fight.

Our church plant was a hard-fought battle that I will always treasure. We did everything we could to keep it financially viable, and it was. We pursued our neighbors with love and served our city with great care, and we saw budding fruit. We created a community; while some did not approve and walked out, many found Jesus there and remained. The work God did in that faith community was good. In fact, as I sit and write about it, I think back so fondly. It might be one of my favorite works of ministry that I was privileged to be part of.

However, due to the approval-based measurements I held our sweet faith community to, I was constantly managing my disappointments. My expectations of attendance numbers, facilities, and options for reaching the city did not measure up to the church we were actually building. It had early seeds sprouting that could have grown into my expectations, but we were running out of steam. Marcus began operating in obligation as though the church was his cross to bear. I had lost vision of how to serve within our realities and couldn't see what could be next. That's when the Lord said, "Stop."

Those words brought a profound wave of peace to my heart, and I had no doubt that what I thought was the beginning was now the end.

In his book, *Necessary Endings*, Henry Cloud writes, "Great is the art of the beginning. But greater is the art of the ending."

I never considered ends to be great. Endings meant losses or failures. But the reality is that if we do not face the fact that some things must end, we will stagnate or even die. I could feel in my heart this was the trajectory for our church if Marcus and I could not come to grips with the fact that it was our time to let go.

We had huge hopes for the future of our church downtown. In our minds, we envisioned a huge skyrise building we would name Hope Center. Of course, in our mind's eye, it would house a vast auditorium that would seat thousands of people every Sunday morning. But that was to be just one of its many amenities. There would be a gymnasium open every day of the week for youth sports and community activities. It would have a juice bar and a coffee shop for people to gather and connect over good food and drink. It would have a swimming pool on one level, because city kids don't have swimming pools in their backyards, and it would be a place to play and learn to swim. It would have clinics to provide for basic physical needs and bring healing. There would be counseling centers, art classes, performing arts, and a hair salon. Hope Center was to be a one-stop-shop to serve the people at the heart of the city, all in Jesus' name.

We believed in our vision so much that Marcus reached out to an architect who attended our church. He asked the man to draw up a rendering of a space like this. After the masterpiece was finished, my husband rolled it out and framed it to hang in his office. Every day he would stare at Hope Center, believing this was the dream God called us to walk out. It was big and inspiring, and we were committed to seeing it fulfilled.

But it never happened. Instead, our church-planting dream ended in resignation—in a necessary ending.

Endings are a part of life. If you want to grab hold of something new, something old must end. It's no wonder it was hard for my heart to dream of new things. It was time for us to move on, leaving behind what we had built before the picture we drew became reality. I had assumed that I would be part of the harvest, but I realized that all God asked us to do was plant.

We could no longer remain because of our fears. We couldn't hang on because of sadness or uncertainty about what our departure would cause. In fact, following the new direction in obedience brought joy to my heart. If I stayed in the way, the whole church could become stuck. I began to believe the truth that Godly endings bring hope.

"If you want to grab hold of something new, something old must end."

The framed architectural plans came down from the office wall when God clearly whispered, "Your time here is up." That's not to say Hope Center won't ultimately come to fruition in this city. Perhaps that is someone else's harvest. Only God knows. But as for us, our planting season was over.

"The Lord will perfect that which concerns me; your mercy, Oh Lord, endures forever; do not forsake the works of Your hands." Psalms 138:8 NKJV

Obedience may feel like a failure—may even look like failure to outsiders—but *perfecting* is what God loves to do. I can confidently say that He is completing a perfecting work in you right now.

During this process, it's okay to grieve expectations. It's not uncommon to feel powerless. It can be traumatic on our brains and hard on our bodies to walk in obedience. It's enormously challenging to our systems when things don't work out the way we hoped. It doesn't make God a liar or mean. It doesn't necessarily mean that we are doing something wrong. But the obedience walk often requires healing along the way and an infusion of hope in the inner parts of our hearts. It will require a release in our spirit that can say with complete confidence, "Lord, I trust you."

"The Lord is my strength and my shield; my heart trusts in him, and he helps me. My heart leaps for joy, and with my song I praise him. The Lord is the strength of his people, a fortress of salvation for his anointed one." Psalm 28:7-8

So, I grieved. I wept over unmet expectations. I had put my misplaced need for a large church on my husband, so I would feel like we mattered and to prove to skeptics in our past that we were great. This proving and striving had to die. I apologized to the Lord and my husband for that. I expressed my sorrow over a desire to pass our church to our son, who would take it in his adulthood to lead. (I'm pretty sure this is not the best parenting to create a plan for your kids, so I left that one at the feet of Jesus that day.) I took responsibility for my desire for a prominent and influential church and for attaching so much of my significance to its success.

For so long, I had walked a road paved with lists of what to do. This new step was a new road and was more about who I would become. I want to embody what Jesus can do in a life when who He is, not just what He does for us, ignites obedience and surrender. As hard as church planting was, our "failure" forced me to wrestle with what success actually means.

That's when I heard a gentler voice whisper to me. It wasn't audible, but it penetrated the deepest parts of my heart. It was a promise from God's Scripture in Proverbs 3:5-6: "Take delight in the Lord, and he will give you the desires of your heart."

Taking delight in the Lord means that our hearts find peace and fulfillment in Him. If we find satisfaction and worth in Christ, Scripture says He will give us the longings of our hearts. This is not translated as "get what you want." It means that when we surrender our hearts to Christ and truly rejoice or "delight" in the eternal things of God, our desires begin to parallel His. What we want will be what He wants, and we will never go unfulfilled.

18

DISCOVERING
YOUR PURPOSE

Addie recently had her senior pictures taken. You know, the ones with the cap and gown? The very thought of it had me in "all the feels." I am sitting in eighteen years of hope, heartache, expectation, disappointment, screaming, silence, care, carrying, belief, and so many moments rattling around in my head and heart.

I remember every win and all the losses.

I recall the kind friends and the patient teachers.

I think back to all the school pick-ups where my heart sank, afraid that this was the day the shoe would drop, and they would tell me she could not come back.

All parents may feel this in some capacity. But the parents of kids with disabilities know exactly what I'm talking about. Yet, in all the exhilarating and terrifying moments, my overarching emotion is delight.

Addie brings me so much delight. She is a joy. Life is so fragile, and it moves me to tears at how much Addie has taught me about humanity. I don't always know if it's going to be okay. I don't always know what to do. But she brings an eternal perspective. She enables me to experience holiness. She brings Heaven to Earth with her childlike faith. Addie keeps me connected to the present moment. I have learned from her how to love well.

She is my calling.

She has helped me see the awe and wonder that is all around me. Addie is a daily reminder of God's goodness, vastness, and beauty.

I'm so grateful for who she is and blown away by what she has done. Honestly, I never doubted her. But the world has, and still does. And because of both her need and her light, tending to her life and advocating for her rights had been my great calling.

Eighteen is not the end. It's just another beginning. But the calling remains.

Significance *is where God is.* Calling is about who we are to "BE" in this world. We all have a call to create beauty around us and to love those in front of us. That can be done anywhere, under any circumstance, and in any context. Tending to what's in front of you well, and bringing goodness into the small things, is part of your calling.

God has designed each of us with great purpose and has promises available to us daily. But so often, we expect life to be linear. We want the results to always be up and to the right. But life includes twists, turns, and even the occasional obscure, obedient place.

How do we find our purpose—our calling—during these twists, especially when we feel like we've lost it?

The first thing you must know is that God *is* calling you. It doesn't matter where you are in your faith journey—your story is important, and you matter. Allowing Christ into our lives through salvation supernaturally activates our calling. Also, the Bible clearly states that calling isn't limited to a select few. It's an invitation to everyone.

Your calling is a gift from God. You don't have to earn it. You also cannot whip it up into meaning on your own. God gave it to you as a gift; it is connected to your salvation.

"He has saved us and called us to a holy life—not because of anything we have done but because of his own purpose and grace." 2 Timothy 1:9

This means that you are not responsible for figuring it all out. Your primary duty is to simply walk it out. I am not called to come up with an excellent plan for my life. God has that part already worked out. Ephesians 2:10 says, "For we are Christ's workmanship created in Christ Jesus, to do good works which He prepared in advance for us to do."

I love the Passion translation of this verse, "We have become his poetry, a re-created people that will fulfill the destiny he has given each of us, for we are joined to Jesus, the Anointed One."

The word "workmanship" in ancient Greek is "poema". This is the word we know in English as "poem". You are God's poem—His divine work of art. There is work to do that is unique to your life. But there is something God desires more than your talent, your work, or even your sacrifice. God wants your heart. You are more valuable than what you do.

This truth has allowed me to be open to my life's twists and turns. There have been seasons I have felt forgotten, as though God picked me up and set me on a shelf. But in those seasons, I have worked through the deep particulars and the broken parts of my own story. I've been healed in the pause of *being* instead of *doing*. I have become whole in the waiting. I have found delight in the delay.

Trusting God's timing leads to a significant life. Wherever you find yourself right now is where you are supposed to be. Hold your head up because where you are right now, today is part of your God-ordained, significant journey.

I'm tired of hearing, "If only I started sooner," or "If I had just launched before her," or "I wish I would have known then...." I get it. I've said all these things, too. But perhaps you weren't ready, and you wouldn't have succeeded like you are now. Any sooner and your circumstances might have caused you to crumble instead of crush it. If you had known then, your heart might not have been ready—it wouldn't have helped you move forward the way it does now.

> God's best rarely follows our proposed path or our perfect timeline.

There is a grand plan; the dream is not in vain. But God's best rarely follows our proposed path or our perfect timeline. And there's an additional challenge baked into the craziness of our modern pace. Our busy schedules usually don't allow us to pause and listen and take inventory of our lives. We rush through our days with an ongoing ache to fulfill our purpose and a low-level terror that we won't. We like to fill in the blanks for God, but we make false assumptions about His promises.

And then, as if that weren't enough, sometimes we suffer.

Suffering does not mean you have missed your calling. In fact, time after time in the pages of the Bible, suffering is a valley we are called to journey through. The "Valley of the Shadow of Death" wasn't a wrong turn on the road to significance. Suffering and sorrow are part of the journey—and God is with us there. Our calling, even in our struggle, is an invitation into alignment with Christ.

Christ Himself suffered. Walking with Him will mean we walk through the struggle too. And in the valley, He shows us who He is. And who we really are.

"For to this you have been called, because Christ also suffered for you, leaving you an example, so that you might follow in his steps." 1 Peter 2:21 ESV

Christ suffered as the Redeemer of a broken world and broken people. We suffer because we live in that broken world and are broken people. Suffering does not deny you the promise of your future. In fact, it refines it—it perfects it.

WE WILL SUFFER BECAUSE WE BEAR THE IMAGE OF CHRIST

If you have made the pursuit of Jesus your highest ambition, you have not missed His will for your life. In fact, that's impossible. You are in it. However wobbly or weary you feel in the journey, God's promise is to order your steps. So, you haven't missed Him.

Christ-like suffering can come in many forms. It's clinging to His provision when all else is falling away. Or trusting in His goodness when loved ones struggle, when dreams are crushed, when diagnoses don't go your way, when trials test your will to live, when life is overwhelming or disappointing. There is no more remarkable testimony than reflecting the image of Christ while suffering is assaulting our lives.

We will suffer along the journey of this life. That's a reality we can't renegotiate. But what we are promised is "presence" in the place of pain: the presence of a loving Savior who has promised to never leave us or forsake us.

"Suffering does not deny you the promise of your future. In fact, it refines it— it perfects it."

WE SUFFER BECAUSE WE SIN

There is no condemnation for those in Christ Jesus. Paul makes this amazing truth abundantly clear in Romans 8:1. We are the beneficiaries of an infinite grace and an astounding redemption. But the fallout of sin, and the wounding that occurs as a natural byproduct of sin, causes suffering throughout the world and in our own stories. Throughout my life as a Christ-follower, I have made choices that clearly indulged my pride and flesh. I've blown it. And the resulting pain inflicted on others and upon my own heart has left scars. Sin inevitably results in suffering.

But suffering is also a divine part of why I have compassion toward people in various situations. Because I understand their pain. I get it. I've suffered like them. And the measure of the comfort I receive from God—His gracious forgiveness, His tender kindness, His powerful presence—is the fullness of the gift of comfort I can extend to others. This is at least part of the purpose in our pain.

To avoid your pain is to avoid your calling because God is up to something in you, and He's going to do something through you. Doing the heart work is necessary and vital. Our sin often requires inner healing. However, that deep work must include our repentance in the process. That's where healing begins. Repentance is the doorway into higher, restored intimacy with God. And the beauty of our Savior is that He is welcoming you with open hands.

But we cannot walk in wholehearted health without owning our own wrongdoing. Without confessing our deep need for Him with radical responsibility, we miss the fulfillment of so much of the promise.

WE SUFFER BECAUSE WE ARE BEING EQUIPPED

Suffering also trains our hearts so that we can accomplish our callings. Suffering is a work of heart-transformation that prepares us for the days ahead. God is shaping and strengthening you for the good work He has prepared for you. Rather than deciphering "why" the suffering might be happening, spend time exploring "what" He could be doing. Then trust that God wants you whole.

His heart for you is *completion*. He's integrating the many parts of your story, weaving the threads of His grace through your life like a Master Craftsman and then exceeding your wildest expectations. In fact, Ephesians 3:20 makes it clear that your mind will be blown.

But here's a truth I really want you to marinade in for a second: you matter. You were explicitly handcrafted by your Creator for such a time as this and for a work like this. God wants to speak to you and use your life for good.

You have an assignment in life. It was custom-made for you. God prepared your destiny in advance and built in all the prerequisites. He installed gifting and skill, dreams, and desires. He wove in personality and uniqueness and capacity for faith. And yes, even our weaknesses as a reminder of how much we need Him.

Some miss this pathway to God's best because they seek something more impressive, or perfect, or worthy of praise and applause. But when they do, they miss something profoundly significant.

Discovering our purpose is not just a fancy way of finding our passion; it's about aligning ourselves with Christ. It's less about achievement or accomplishment and more about our divine connection with Him. Our purpose is the process of entering God's plan.

We often put God in a box, and then search outside for clues about who we're supposed to be. Or, in our desire to live life on purpose, we're afraid to get it wrong. We don't want to miss God's good for us or, even worse, be a disappointment to Him. These are flawed ways to look at the purposes of God for your life. Our identity is made *in* Him, prepared in advance. We won't miss it. We can't.

The history of the word "call" in the Christian community comes from the Latin "vocare" or "voice," meaning to follow the voice of God. In modern terms, it is our "vocation" that enables us to connect our God-given gifts and passions with God's mission on earth. According to Frederick Buechner, "The place God calls you is the place where your deep gladness and the world's deep hunger meet."[4]

That intersecting point is your calling, your vocation.

Vocation and calling are the exact words, one from Latin and one from Greek. It represents the voice we desire so deeply to discover and live out confidently. Vocation is the deeper meaning that our soul cries out for. It is the longer story of one's life, commitments, passions, gifts, skills, loves, and longings that make us uniquely "us."

Vocation is altogether separate from your occupation. Your occupation describes the relationships and responsibilities along the way of life that we "occupy." God uses occupations to prepare us and refine us, but they will shift and change and do not define our core worth or identity. This is often where we get stuck.

It was a great challenge for me to understand my purpose over the years, as my roles and responsibilities changed. I am a wife. I am a mom. I am a salon receptionist. I am a retail salesperson. I am an administrator. I am a pastor's wife. I am a health coach. I am a business leader. And (my deepest desire) I am significant because I am using my voice to change the world.

This deep truth gave me great comfort in my ever-changing roles. And it also empowered my steps into every place God led me. Occupations come and go. Vocations are ours for life.

---

[4] Buechner, Frederick. Wishful Thinking: A Theological ABC. Harper & Row, 1973.

In the "now-but-not-yet" world that is ours, there's always a dissonance between what we feel we were made for and what we do daily. In everyone's life, there is a lack of harmony. *This cannot be it. But wait, in the past, I have been like this. Now I am doing this. And yet, for whatever reason, I can no longer do this.* This dissonance can lead to feeling lost.

Part of my confusion along the road to living out my purpose was that I needed clarification about how purpose was attained. So when the occupations or roles I played shifted and changed, I sometimes felt like I had missed it. I had talents and abilities that would be used in different ways and spaces, but that did not equal fulfillment of my calling. My thinking was often so black and white with no room for flexibility, partly because I thought I was primarily responsible for achieving my purpose on my own.

Instead, I have discovered that living out your purpose has one requirement: *surrender.* Giving God permission to bring you out-of-the-box invitations is essential. You need to let God have the freedom to *be* God in your life. Our instinct is to view His surprise opportunities as competition to what we're doing. But God can make all things compatible.

This was one of the biggest hang-ups for me personally. When I first moved into the business world, I felt confused. I had always held positions doing church ministry work and incorrectly equated ministry with my purpose. Eventually, I understood that the local church was a *vehicle* that enabled my purpose—and that business was *another* vehicle to do the same. It was not my vocation that changed but my occupation. This new awareness set my heart free from the confines of whatever work I put my hands to doing. If I pursued *Him* as my path, it would be impossible to miss His plan.

If you are a Christian or have experience in church, it can be common to divide work into sacred and secular spaces. But this is a false construct. I am a carrier of the light and hope of Christ, a Kingdom carrier.

Kingdom carriers are business owners, bakers, doctors, teachers, lawyers, engineers, and designers. And if we are to fulfill our Biblical mandate to go into all the world and share the wonderful news of the Gospel openly with the entire human race, then we must shift our perspective. Kingdom work does not only happen in church services, on stages, or on street corners. Kingdom work is happening when I open my mind and surrender my heart. It's where I join God in reshaping the world through ordinary places like homes, school pick-up lines, fitness centers, social media, Target stores, neighborhood gatherings, and all the places I have connected with the thousands of people in my business.

> *One sure thing: your calling is connected to others.*

I recently asked a sisterhood group I lead on Facebook how they would define significance. Surprisingly, the responses were overwhelmingly connected to others, not to occupations. They were words like *seen, chosen, valued, difference-maker, special, elevated,* and *making a difference in the world.*

One sure thing: your calling is connected to others. You cannot fulfill your purpose in life by yourself. You can only do it connected with other people.

Don't miss it. God ordains your ordinary, scattering His beloved servants all over the workplace. Hold loosely the identity you gained when you received that degree as you walked across that stage. Don't cling too hard to the path that got you where you are today. The road may curve to get you where God wants to lead you for your tomorrow. I encourage you to get your soul clear on who you are and who you are not.

FINALLY, YOUR CALLING IS PERMANENT

I'm so glad about this one. It doesn't matter how messed up your life has been. If you messed it up, or if someone messed it up for you—your calling doesn't change. God has no plan B for you or for me. Your messy past doesn't modify God's call on your life. In fact, the mess makes you *you*, and so often it's part of how God uses you in the life of another.

"Before I shaped you in the womb, I knew all about you.
Before you saw the light of day, I had holy plans for you."
Jeremiah 1:5 MSG

The Bible says that you were custom-made in Heaven. God says He shaped and knew you; He had holy plans for you before you were born. You were no accident. Your life is not by chance. God has a sovereign, holy ambition for you.

As I type these words, I pray your heart will swell with incredible hope. This may be a revolutionary concept depending on the story you've been told or the road you've traveled. Regardless of your day, the discouragement you're experiencing, or the struggles you're going through, God has a calling on your life. He set it in place before time began; it's already working its way out. And that calling is not going anywhere.

19

LET GOD WORK THE BIG THINGS

Don't you just love something that far exceeds your expectations? I've been pleasantly surprised by restaurants with better food than I thought they'd have. I've checked into vacation hotels that blew my mind. And there's nothing better than going in expecting three stars and getting five.

As great as it is to have something surpass your wildest expectations, when expectations aren't met, it's downright deflating. Frankly, I prefer the highlight reel. The wins. Successes and achievements. That's what I want to share. I like it when life is looking up, and things are going my way.

But disappointment is as much a part of life as the highlight reel.

My youngest daughter, Piper, is incredibly precocious, just like her name. She is smart, witty, independent, and fiercely competitive in martial arts. I can brag because I can't take much credit for the above.

My incredibly determined girl competes in her craft of martial arts. She has been esteemed in her class and quickly rose through the ranks. Most things come easy for her. However, recently Piper began to come up against brick walls in her training. It was as though everything she attempted felt like a fail. The competition was fierce, and my precious baby girl was buckling under intense pressure.

After a series of disappointingly low competition rankings and an inability to complete specific requirements to move up in her class, she finally broke down. She was displeased with her performances and utterly disheartened.

I grabbed her blubbering, sweet cheeks and looked her square in the face to tell her the truth about disappointment. I peered into her eyes and validated every emotion she had at that moment. I soothed her feelings with the most enormous embrace only a mother can give. Then I looked back into those teary eyes and said, "Count it all joy, sweet thing."

If this seems counter-intuitive, it's because it is.

"Consider it pure joy, my brothers and sisters, whenever you face trials of many kinds because you know that the testing of your faith produces perseverance. Let perseverance finish its work so that you may be mature and complete, not lacking anything." James 1:2-4

I, too, have wrestled with a sense of loss and the feeling of not being good enough. Incessantly. Whether it be a business goal I didn't reach or an unfulfilled ministry expectation, I have found disappointment transformative. Disappointment is never welcome, but it can also pack a powerful purpose. Disappointment has been the catalyst for many dreams and achievements in my life. The victory is won when we don't stop. It's when we take our thinking beyond ourselves and expand our mindset so that it's fixed on God.

When something doesn't go our way, we are often consumed by the horrible feelings it produces. You can concentrate on your failures or focus on your future. After counting it all joy, you must develop a stronger conviction than your condition. You must be so anchored to your belief and the hope of possibility that it drives you through the present circumstance. That often requires a shift in perspective. What you dwell on will drown you if your perspective isn't rooted in truth.

Recognize the failing for what it is.

So, you didn't get the promotion. You didn't get published. You didn't make the cut. In Piper's case, she messed up and didn't win. But adversity doesn't have to stop us from advancing. Suffering doesn't mean we need to stop. If you focus on what you can learn, you can move forward. The setback could catalyze your comeback.

I won't deny that disappointment can profoundly impact our relationship with God. When things didn't go my way in the early years, I blamed myself. "This must be my fault," so I hustled for more. I self-bullied and then grinded to make myself worthy.

But as I experienced more disappointment in my later years, I have gotten angry with God. My anger would come in the form of aggressive protests, beginning with the list of everything I do:

* I'm serving You, Lord.
* I've put You first.
* I have sacrificed.
* I love Your people even when they don't love me back.
* I'm prioritizing You above all else.

It would then turn to angry questions:

* How can You do this?
* Why would You? I have surrendered to You; I have submitted to You.

* How could You not work things out the way I think You should?

I sat with these questions for years. When dreams, adventures, and the church didn't work out the way I told God it should, I was disappointed. But this pain was a catalyst for my change, and it matured my life and faith.

*"Surrender your anxiety. Be still and realize that I am God.
I am God above all the nations, and I am exalted throughout
the whole earth. 'Here he stands! The Commander!
The mighty Lord of Angel Armies is on our side!
The God of Jacob fights for us! Pause in his presence.'"*
Psalm 46:10-11 TPT

I used to take this psalm as a pep talk for my soul: *I get it, Lord. You want me to pause. I'll give You the nod, acknowledge Your ability, and take a minute to rest before I get up and go back in.*

But it's more than a pep talk. God shifts our trajectory when we put our hands down and palms up. I cannot manufacture all the outcomes of my life. I pursue good things. I have goals, dreams, and checklists to get it all done. But now I recognize that *process* is the biggest piece of the puzzle that works God's purpose out in me.

This psalm gives me the command to stop my futile effort in the things that are God's domain. It's not about some specific outcome or destination; it's the road along the way. In fact, incredible outcomes, ones I didn't expect and could have only hoped for, have come because I trusted Him, setting one foot in front of the other.

If God always met our expectations, He would never have the opportunity to exceed them. It doesn't matter where you are in your story. It doesn't matter if you want to fight or flee in your highs and lows. It doesn't matter if you think you count or not. Your significance is not connected to external circumstances or even your spiritual gifting. You matter because you belong to God. That is what makes your life count. Not who you are, but *whose* you are.

Embrace the hard so you can live out hope. This release of control—to trust—enables you to be still and know He is God.

A few days after one of Piper's "losing streak" competitions, an email was sent out. It was from her head sensei to all the competitors and said, "For those of you who won, congratulations. You have successfully continued a long tradition of winning and excellence. Now let me say this. You will not always win! That is a one hundred percent guarantee. In fact, you will lose way more than you will win. Losing is fuel. Winning is fuel. Everything is fuel!"

Joy and suffering are inseparably linked and of great eternal value. The Lord brings them into our lives as we need them and for His great purposes. Embrace both. Waste neither.

Faith is rarely a spectator sport. Jesus loves to see our faith in action.

Piper takes big risks for being tiny. She braves the unknown when she says yes to putting her abilities, hard work, and determination on the gym floor to compete. She does her best. And you get the same invitation. The risks you take, the attempts you make, and the fears you walk through all put you one step closer to realizing what you want. Everything is fuel.

The Bible is full of miracles where a person, at the point of their deepest need, experienced their greatest blessing when they depended on God. God wants us to participate in the miracle He is doing; sometimes that participation requires action. The truth is that faith works, so work your faith.

"Just as the body is dead without breath, so also faith is dead without good works." James 2:26 NLT

"Embrace the <u>hard</u> so you can live out <u>hope</u>."

This is not about earning your faith or working harder for it. This is about faith *that works*. Your faith is effective when it is in action. God loves sending water, but sometimes He asks you to dig a ditch to put it in. Faithfulness is grabbing your shovel and rolling up your sleeves.

In 2 Kings, three kings set out to take over the Moabites. After a roundabout march of seven days, the army had no more water for themselves or the animals with them. Scripture tells us that these guys thought this would be an easy battle. They weren't prepared for it to be this hard. They expected it to be a walk in the park. Instead, it turned out to be a grind through Death Valley.

"Has the Lord called us three kings together only to deliver us into the hands of *Moab?*" they cried out.

Basically, they were saying, "These guys? Are you kidding me? You bring us all the way out here in the desert just to let us die of thirst and get our rears kicked by these pushovers?"

Ever felt that way? *But God, I obeyed You. I am following Your commands. I trusted You. I thought this was going to be easier. I'm all in, but for this? This wasn't on my list. This isn't what I signed up for.*

I have said these words a few times. And thought them even more.

These three kings sought out a prophet. Not just any prophet, but a guy with street cred. His name was Elisha. And Elisha came from what I consider "shock and awe" stock. He was the former apprentice of Elijah. Back in the day, Elijah had called upon God to deliver a full-blown downpour of rain from the tiniest of clouds during a terrible drought. I imagine these guys thinking, "We need water, so go get the Rain Maker's Apprentice."

And so it was that Elisha agreed to call out to God on their behalf. But the answer is different from what they expected.

"He then said, 'God's word: Dig ditches all over this valley.
Here's what will happen—you won't hear the wind, you won't
see the rain, but this valley is going to fill up with water
and your army and your animals will drink their fill.'"
2 Kings 3:16-17 MSG

These men are dying of thirst, and the command that comes back is to dig some ditches. Do manual labor in the hot desert sun. Do you really think the God of the universe needed these troops to dig ditches? No. But sometimes God wants us to show Him our faith, so He can show us His faithfulness.

> *Sometimes God wants us to show Him our faith, so He can show us His faithfulness.*

The steps of faithfulness are often small, but they prepare the way for big things. Work the little things like they are big, and God will work the big things like they are little. Grab a shovel and go after the part you can do, and God will take care of the part you can't.

The size of your dream doesn't intimidate God. The size of your need doesn't worry Him in the least. But sometimes you need to stop waiting and start working. Your effort might seem insignificant, but as Zechariah 4:10 says, "Do not despise the day of small beginnings."

How do you dig a ditch? One shovel of dirt at a time. Keep going. Little by little.

The Enemy of our soul believes in our purpose and potential more than we sometimes do. And that's a tragedy. He tries to discourage our pursuit of Jesus by overwhelming us with pressure to put God's responsibility on our shoulders or with the suffering that can come with change. It's time to counterpunch by following the Giver of the promise in our everyday steps. Look what God did for those kings in the desert:

"The next morning, about the time for offering the sacrifice, there it was—water flowing from the direction of Edom! And the land was filled with water." 2 Kings 3:20

There it is, God delivering what only He can provide. So, keep expecting. No matter how hard it gets or how risky it feels. Put your faith into action and dig your ditch. Trust that at just the right time, there will come (out of nowhere) precisely what God said He would do to meet your greatest need out of His inexhaustible supply.

Work the little things like they are big, and God will work the big things like they are little. And you will receive His surprise.

20

THE POWER OF PERHAPS

If you had asked me years ago what kind of mom I would be to a teen driver, I would have responded with, "I won't."

Of course, I would have been joking. Kind of.

In truth, the thought of my kids taking the driver's seat on the freeways of Southern California and proactively putting themselves in a position to get run over was totally lost on me. *Why would any good mom be okay with that?*

And then the day came. My second daughter was turning sixteen, and it was all she could do not to completely lose her mind because she was so excited to get that driver's license. Her reasoning challenged me even more. It was a desire for greater independence. She wanted more autonomy from her dad, her siblings, and me. That statement alone would have put me to bed for the night in the past.

What did I do wrong? I'm a super fun mom. Do you realize the responsibility that comes with driving? Don't you just feel better with me figuring everything out?

But not anymore. Through all my practice at letting go, I saw that what Tatum desired was appropriate. The season of more independence was coming for her, and it was necessary for her development and personal growth. She should want to spread her wings at sixteen. For many people, sixteen is a celebration of womanhood and marks the end of a girl's childhood.

Who was I to rob my girl of this monumental moment? Who was I to say what should make her feel afraid or cause her to feel safe? And so, the second she got her permit, I decided to hop in the passenger seat and brave the freeway without screeching. (I didn't even grab the handle above my side door window once.)

> *Yes is exciting.*
> *Yes leads to more.*
> *But yes can also*
> *feel risky.*

I'll admit that driving is dangerous. I mean, we take rush hour to a whole new level. But more dangerous is stifling my daughter because of fears that have nothing to do with her. Trust enabled me to say "YES!"

I think it's fun to say "yes". Yes, you can go. Yes, you can have that. Yes, we can do it.

Yes is exciting. *Yes* leads to more. But *yes* can also feel risky. It's scary to live out sometimes, like when precious teenage daughters drive on precarious freeways.

No is easier for lots of reasons. We say "no" because we have been burned. We have been disappointed. We have been rejected. We say "no" because we've all experienced pain, loss, and failure. These real-life experiences muffle our *yes* and amplify our *no*.

"Not this time, not again. I can't. I won't! NO!"

But we can experience an audacity that refuses to accept *no* as our de facto attitude. And here's the thing about audacity: it's the willingness to take bold risks. It's daring fearlessness. It's courage and grit. There is a word that has enabled me to dance in the nuance of less control and more trust. It is one small but powerful word. It's the word "perhaps". I'll return to it in a minute, but first a story.

It was summer and my two oldest daughters, Addie and Tatum, had the chance to attend our church summer camp. Since both were now teenagers, it was that next-level kind of youth camp with more independence, all-night adventures, and cool, college-age chaperones.

I wanted to say "yes" for so many reasons. Summer camps changed my life. The encounters I had with God at chapel each night honestly saved me. I wanted this experience for all my kids. Tatum was an easy decision. But how would this work out for Addie? She has been fully included in most environments and is capable in many respects. But she had never successfully stayed overnight at any youth events without the assistance of Mom, Dad, or Grandma.

But here's the thing: my deepest desire for Addie has always been her independence. I want her to grow into the full potential God had in mind when He made her. I don't want to limit her abilities by being a "hover mother" who makes decisions for her out of fear.

Sending Addie to camp would require me to do a challenging thing. It was more than a little scary for me to let her go. Health and safety are a thing for any child. And just a little extra of a thing for her. So the night before camp, with all the family gathered around, I said, "Addie, I don't think you can go to camp." Her face dropped. My other kids gasped. "Why not, Mom!? Why can't Addie go to camp?"

The truth was that *no* was just easier. It just rolled out of my frightened heart and over my anxious lips without any effort at all.

No meant I didn't have to overcome my worry. It meant I could feel more in control. It seemed safe. But *no* would also mean no growth. It would mean no opportunity to reach new heights. *No* to overcoming, *no* to something extraordinary.

A little later that night Addie passed me a little note, scribbled in her distinctive penmanship, that read, "I want to go to camp, please."

Perhaps I had missed it. Maybe I had something to learn. Perhaps there was a good thing here that my *no* never saw coming. My heart sank through the floor, but something new suddenly began to rise. I turned to my husband. As he glanced at the words of this precious little note, I took a deep sigh—knowing what was right.

The answer should be "yes"! It's a daring *yes*. And it was the right answer all along. *Yes* to lifting lids of possibility. *Yes* to getting uncomfortable in the face of fear. "YES!"

No is the breeding ground of fear. But *yes* leads to the possibility of what life can become.

Control keeps us comfortable. But I don't want to play it safe. Not for me or on behalf of my children. I want to play to win. That's the difference between fear and faith. If fear dictates your decisions, you are on the defense, reactive, and cautious. But making decisions by faith means pushing past all of that and going on the offensive in life.

Faith moves God. He absolutely loves it. It pleases Him. When our *yes* is motivated for His glory, it moves His heart and His hand. Is it daring? Yes. Is it worth it? Absolutely.

1 Samuel tells the story of a man named Jonathan. He was the oldest son of King Saul. He is first mentioned in 1 Samuel 13 when he defeated a patrol of Philistines. My Bible describes the scene as "Jonathan's daring plan."

To catch you up a bit, the Philistines controlled the border of Israel as bullies in the geographical neighborhood. And for whatever reason,

King Saul seemed content to sit on the sideline of the skirmish. But Jonathan wanted to be on the front lines.

He said to his armor-bearer, "Come, let's go over to the Philistine outpost on the other side." As much as his dad was good at saying "no," Jonathan desired more than the status quo. He was born for more. He was made for *yes*.

And so, he devised a plan to confront his adversaries. And his strategy was risky. Jonathan would cross over to the Philistine fortress, navigating sharp rocky cliffs on either side. He planned to expose himself in broad daylight to the enemy, clearly conceding the high ground. And in verse 8, we pick up the story: Jonathan said, "Here's what we'll do. We'll cross over the pass and let the men see we're there."

What compels this kind of courage? What suppressed his fear and fueled his faith?

Jonathan reveals it all in a powerful verse, which got me thinking. He said, "Perhaps the Lord will act on our behalf."

Perhaps.

He chose to believe that perhaps God would work for him. And that one little word is a big statement of faith. We often operate with the opposite mindset. *What if he doesn't? Perhaps he won't.*

That's your fear working, not your faith. And all bravery needs is one tiny "perhaps". *Perhaps* is the springboard towards *yes*. It's the manifestation of our trust. And one *yes* can change not only your destiny but an entire family, community, or nation. A daring *yes* is reaching just beyond your perimeters and can change the world.

In fact, that is precisely what happened with Jonathan. With one *perhaps*, he scaled that cliff, confronted his adversaries, and conquered the entire garrison of Philistines. And "so on that day," verse 23 tells us, "the Lord saved Israel."

What a day!

So, what about Addie? My sweet teenage daughter went to camp. She went away for the entire four days and three nights. And she did it all by herself. Did she survive? Yes. But far more than that, she thrived. Our *yes* to trust and release of control cultivated incredible confidence in our remarkable girl. She had fun, deepened friendships, and took a further step toward her God-given destiny. Our church held water baptisms down at the beach the weekend after she came home from camp. And who decided to take her personal faith public? You guessed it, Addie.

When I asked her why, she gave a simple yet profound response, "Jesus is in my heart. I want to tell people. I'm a teenager, Mom; I'm ready." This is what it means to expand your faith. This is the legacy of a daring *yes* and the power of *perhaps*.

> *Nothing about God is predictable. The Holy Spirit is uncontainable.*

When we are handcuffed by *no*, when we are stuck in a box defined by how "it's supposed to be," we miss out on fully living. Having integrity, seeking wisdom, getting educated, and growing your skills are important. But the problem is when all of these rules of engagement become idols and stifle your ability to trust God.

Nothing about God is predictable. The Holy Spirit is uncontainable. Just say "*yes*" and take the next step. Have dreams. Make all the plans. This is the starting point. And then trust the God who created you. Your authority comes from Him. Your future is not attached to a paved path, a predictable plan, or all the appropriate steps. Your power comes from the King of kings. So imagine what He can do outside of the "control" box.

Life is full of possibilities. One *yes* can be the catalyst. One little *perhaps* can be the hope, the daring affirmation that leads to a life "exceedingly, abundantly above and beyond whatever you ask, think or imagine," according to Ephesians 3.

Don't remain handcuffed by *no*. *Perhaps* there's a *yes* in your future. Audaciously take the leap and go.

Section 4

COMMUNITY

21

WHEN FRIENDSHIPS BREAK

At the beginning of our church planting, I feared I would be alone. Of course, I had my husband and our four kids. But after what happened with the layoff, we had low expectations for friendships with adults. Many of our "close" friendships had grown awkward and distant in the days that followed our departure.

Most on the outside had no idea of the daily torment I was living in. They weren't all bad days, but it was hard. The moments of profound difficulty were things I was scared to share. My intent was not to be phony, but I didn't feel safe in most circles. I found myself in relationships that didn't fully know me, or I assumed they couldn't.

But to my surprise, I made a friend during this season. In some ways, she felt safer than just any friend. She was a person from our history. Someone we had a mutual connection with in our old neighborhood. She had moved from the burbs and was enjoying the city. I was eager to talk and connect and ask her all of my questions. Our sameness in story drove us close quickly, and after our first lunch together, she jumped at the chance to join our family in launching our church.

I loved her wholeheartedly. We shared a lot of good times. I called her a "refrigerator friend." She was the kind of friend who would drop by unannounced and help herself to whatever was in the fridge. I loved it. I was honored, and I knew I could do the same.

We had a lot of heart-to-hearts about God. She was hungering for His freedom, and we dove deep into His word. We hosted parties and small groups. We jogged together in our neighborhood and had prayer walks. Nothing was off limits. We covered it all. We talked about ministry and family. We shared heavy stuff, like the pains of our pasts and the big dreams for the future. Sometimes, we laughed until we cried. Sometimes we'd cry until we laughed. We did life over tasty food and fun fashion. She became the friend with whom I didn't second guess my words or feel the need to filter my responses. I could call her for anything at any time. She was my "go-to" girl.

Until one day she just wasn't. The bonds that had held us so close, were now broken. And now, so was my heart.

I let her in so close. I trusted her. I risked a lot by being vulnerable with her. I had thought that I was seen; but then, unexpectedly, I was rejected. The bridge I never thought would burn was now on fire.

I heard Christine Caine once say, "Perhaps there is no greater pain between friends than the pain of being seen and then unexpectedly rejected."

When she cut me off and walked away, I didn't know how to respond. It was as though the wind got knocked out of me. I was just gasping to catch my breath. As is my tendency, my temptation was to toughen up. To harden my heart and build a wall, so that no one could ever hurt me like that again. I do believe God made us for relationships, and friendship is one of His greatest gifts to us. He created us for connection—connecting to Him and building community with one another. But as much as friendships had helped me, like this "breakup" was, they hurt me as well.

While there are two sides to every relationship breakup, a piece of each heart feels "it's not fair." And maybe it isn't. But to replace destructive cycles with lasting changes, we must empty ourselves of the lie that other people or things can fill our hearts. We must intentionally and consistently fill up on truth and stand secure in God's love.

Of course, this is easier said than done. There are big chunks of my story that are connected to relational conflict. I love people deeply. I have given my life to prove this fact. And while I often have had great intentions, I have also messed things up along the way. I have made it my mission to create good friendships and prided myself on never burning bridges.

> *We must intentionally and consistently fill up on truth and stand secure in God's love.*

Still, somewhere along the way, I picked up a skewed savior complex. I took on a role that said it's my job to fix others. *I'm responsible for their "better way."* It sounds so silly even as I type it, but it was an attempt to control and a way to be seen as worthy, especially in my circle. This was challenging because not everyone in my circle approved.

In fact, some women in my ministry had opinions about my decisions. There were women who wanted to be connected, yet they also questioned me and my passion and successes with statements like, "Who does she think she is?"

These women wanted the "old Jen."

But this was Jen. This is Jen. All of me.

This is Jen following God with a burning in her belly to serve Jesus loudly and boldly without hesitation or restriction. All because of the incredible healing and wholeness He has delivered to my life. I didn't want to go alone. I would have loved everyone to join me. But my invitation to a divinely different life brought incredible discomfort to that circle. Things were changing because I had grown, and that meant the circle would look different because I was different. My life was moving in a new direction, which was God's plan. They loved me. They just didn't understand.

For the longest time, I took this personally. I minimized my strengths and the boldness of my vision to change the world. I attempted to help them understand me better by bringing them into my dream board sessions and vision casting exercises, only to be met with judgment and criticism.

Eventually, I had to face the reality that those I was hanging with did not approve of this growth in me. They didn't enjoy the "elevated" Jen nearly as much as I was enjoying what God was doing in me. They loved me and were able to celebrate some of my success; but when I continued to pursue my passions and purposes, it caused discomfort. They wanted me to stay small.

I heard Lisa Whittle say, "Sometimes your greatest heartache will be that people you love won't want to go to the same places you know God is leading you." Her encouragement: go anyway.

I was forced to make decisions at that moment, and so were they. No bridges burned, but I had to look closely at where God was leading me and ask myself how much time and proximity I would continue to invest with this crew.

Obedience sometimes creates tension like this. I can think of times when my voice was muted when people said I was "getting too big for my britches" just because what I was saying or doing was impactful or influential. This rejection was painful, but it invited me to acknowledge an important truth about myself: I needed and wanted approval from others.

The problem was that my obedience was causing me to lose approval and even friendships. Not everyone thought my growth was great. Not everyone was applauding from the stands. Some preferred me to stay small, to live a normal life without aspirations for more. They wanted me to be grateful for our little circle without stretching beyond.

I think this can be a big deal in Christian church culture—we'll elevate people with particular gifts or talents, but after a minute or two, we're telling that same person to dial it back. Don't want to be "prideful" or "self-aggrandizing." We sometimes over-spiritualize when someone is going for it; likewise, we spiritualize when they are holding back.

But if I was going to fulfill my purpose, I would have to let go of the need to be admired by all and live solely for the audience of one—Jesus. I cannot go to all the places I need to go, nor say all the things I need to say, if I go at this life without Him. So when I am distracted by people's disapproval, or realize I am being unfriended because I am misunderstood, He keeps me rooted. When I question, He gives me perspective. When I am weak, He can do miracles beyond my strength.

The truth is, obediently going for it and living out who you are, loudly and boldly, will eventually trigger someone else's insecurity or scarcity mindset. And what's the first thing they do when triggered? They sneer and point at you and want you to sit down.

When this happens, it's easy to fall into the trap of believing that you only have two choices: live lonely or attempt to please everybody. Neither option is God's best for us, but losing friendships or being misunderstood may make it seem like your options are limited.

How do we work through all of this?

Here's how. We learn to navigate relational failure, then give ourselves permission to grieve. Your strength will never come without these divine moments of rejection and defeat. This is the becoming process. This is when you get to choose to let Him take His rightful place in your life. He is God, and you are not. It's a progression of trust. The most significant moments of our lives are connected to other humans, and it's hard to trust when we have been hurt. But a significant life stems from a surrendered heart—a heart that says I will give more and expect less. I will walk into circles with nothing to prove, only something to give.

I want you to know that the people you are meant to ride with will not have to be convinced of your worth. So, release the others and loosen the grip of control. Our identity is not in people's approval but in knowing who we are in Christ. This enables us to lead a life that is loaded with intention. It allows God to do what He wants instead of being limited by what others see.

I read recently, "You are your sister's keeper, but not her copy." It's time to understand that your obedience is incompatible with people-pleasing. We must submit to what we know God is calling us to. That will stretch us with a few new hello's and will include a few goodbyes.

You may lose some people, but they aren't the right people. Who we hang with cannot include people threatened by our growth and consistency because our path is different. We will need to create boundaries and learn to let go. This will make room for those who are the right people and create a margin for the mission God has purposed for us.

The rewards of this difficult decision are the joys of rich friendships with the right people.

"A significant life stems from a surrendered heart— a heart that says I will give more and expect less."

22

MOM GUILT

When we moved into the city, we lived less than a block up the hill from the school entrance. In my mind this was ideal. I envisioned our home being the after school stop for popsicles. I could see us blocking off the road, playing games with all the families in the neighborhood until the streetlights went out. I loved the convenience and hoped to immerse ourselves in this new community with the school being our starting block.

In the suburbs, going to the neighborhood school meant some things. For starters, it meant high test scores. It meant involved parents with higher education degrees themselves. It meant the best teachers in town and the greatest resources to support them. It meant opportunity for challenge and growth because the bar was set very high. It meant everything at our fingertips for my three neurotypical children and the best access for our daughter with Down syndrome.

Naively, I assumed our new neighborhood school in the city would offer the same things, or at least close. Here's what I didn't know:

* 51% of the student body were English language learners,

* Only 41% of parents were high school graduates,

* On a one-to-ten scale, this school has been graded a two,
* They did not achieve their academic progress index target,
* And while there are many opinions on test scores and how schools are ranked, I think it's safe to say ours was considered a low-performing academic environment.

Once I got a more accurate picture of what we had enrolled our kids in, I was anxious. I'll never forget Day One. We got to the black top and had our kids line up with the rest of their classmates. We waited and we all stared at each other.

I had a pit in my gut. There were no morning announcements from the hype squad of educators. No back-to-school welcome. No PTA refreshment tables. All I was surrounded by on Day One was an immense sense of apathy on this campus. It overwhelmed me. The despair that hovered over the playground was so thick, it was hard to escape. But I tried.

Marcus and I silently walked the half block back up the hill to our home. As we reached our driveaway, I broke the ice by saying, "I have to go. I can't stay here. I'm going to my old small group. This reality is too much to bear." So I called a friend and asked if I could show up to Bible study in thirty minutes. "Of course," she said. "Everything all right?"

"No! It's not. I'll tell you all when I get there."

Upon arrival, I burst into tears. I couldn't even pull myself together enough to create a clear sentence. I was way beyond streaming mascara; I had snot dripping down to the ground as I hunched over with groans, crying from the deepest place.

What have I done to my kids? Will this ruin them? I can't believe this is happening. I am a good mom. Why am I doing this to them? Mom guilt. It crushed me. It began to eat away my hopes to the very core. It caused me to doubt every decision I had ever made and completely robbed me of my joy.

I spent many sleepless nights staring at the ceiling. Just about everyone advised us to flee the city school. "Bad education!" they cried. They encouraged doing what was in the "best interest" of our kids.

They expressed concerns for their safety.

"Children shouldn't pay the price for their parent's convictions," they said.

I listened. I researched. I advocated. I toured. And while I applied to every good school in the city, the circumstances for my kids grew increasingly worse. The resources for Addie were sparse, in part because most of the kids in her class had Individual Education Plans with behavioral support. She quickly got lost in the shuffle and I was terrified that her previous years of progress would be lost.

We hired an advocate. We wrote letters to the district superintendent. We met with the teachers. I brought coffee to the principal. We weren't mad; we were deeply concerned. There had to be better options for every child in this school. But with shrugged shoulders and surrendered hands, the administrators showed us that this fight was an uphill climb. My kids would likely never see the desired outcomes of my advocacy, and perhaps it was best if we tried to move on.

As the school year drew to a close, we decided to explore other options. We submitted applications to our top four local charter schools and prayed.

The demand for charter schools was much greater than the supply, but we were thrilled when the entrance lottery took place and Addie was picked. Of all my kids who needed a rescue, Addie was number one. This was incredible news, but it didn't seal the deal; my two other grade school children remained on the waiting list.

Then, just before school was to begin, we received word that our second oldest, Tatum, had secured a spot in third grade. Now all we needed was a place for Brody. We prayed. We believed we begged. But there was no room for Brody.

Like many parents, I tried to manipulate the system, but I quickly discovered that there was no more I could do. Brody remained in the neighborhood school and experienced everything I dreaded. He had his first encounter with a bully in the bathroom. He cried. He played sick. He behaved in ways I'd never seen before. I began to believe that Brody's suffering was all my fault. *Mom guilt again.* It takes so many forms:

* Should I do this for my child? She did that.

* Does my kid need those? They seem to.

* Look over here; look over there.

* It worked for them; will it work for us?

* Is that what my child should do?

* Will that make me a better mom?

* If we are like that, will it mean I am good?

This is the crazy chatter that so often goes on inside a mom's head. There is a deafening noise on *how* to mother, *when* to mother, *who* to mother; and it seems as though we can never get it all coordinated. Just when I thought I got it right for my oldest girls, I was pretty sure I messed up my only son!

To put this chatter to rest, we try all sorts of tricks. We make lists of pros and cons for our kids. We seek the advice of experts. We try to tap into our intuition, our instincts, our experiences. And while God created us with incredible insight for the babies we carried and birthed, I confess I don't always know what to do.

Having guilt as a mom is real. It's a bully and it never fights fair. Just when we are down, it kicks us again below the belt. Guilt will mess you up if you believe its lies. Part of our attempt to control outcomes as they relate to our kids is because of this big bully. It will chew you up and spit you out. We hold on so tightly to never mess up and to prevent our kids from ever doing wrong either.

In our vulnerability, it's tempting to look around and measure our success by someone else's yardstick. This comparison game of motherhood, especially coupled with mom guilt, takes even the best of us down quickly. The constant dialogue that comes from looking around can make your head spin.

That was exactly the space I found myself in with my children. My biggest concern with our move was always for their welfare. They were old enough to make formative memories, and I was afraid that they would be the kind of memories they would later recall as traumatic. I felt so much pressure to keep that from happening. Fortunately, God was there to help.

He reminded me that progress, not perfection, is the goal. This is the core of what it means to be a Christian. The focus is not me, but Christ. It's not what I can pull off, perform, or proclaim. It's all about Jesus. The hard parts are on Him. It's not that my efforts don't matter—I have free will and make choices. It's just that my best endeavors are to be just an overflow of intimacy with Jesus.

Having guilt as a mom is real.

Just like being a perfect Christian, being a perfect parent is impossible. And yet, when I live a life of absolute surrender and constant dependence upon God, the impossible life becomes possible. I live not out of my own resources and strength; but Jesus, through the indwelling of the Holy Spirit in my life, brings it about. This reality, more than anything, radically reduced my mom guilt.

Paul writes in Galatians 2:20, "I have been crucified with Christ; it is no longer I who live, but Christ lives in me; and the life which I now live in the flesh I live by faith in the Son of God, who loved me and gave Himself for me."

This is a life of faith in Jesus. This is the path to less pressure and more passion in the call of mothering.

Faith isn't some mystical concept that I say I have. Faith is expressed in action. Faith is the realization that the life God is calling me to is impossible to do perfectly. I can't love the way I'm called to. I can't live above the power of sin. I can't treat people the way Jesus would. I can't always have a guard upon my mouth. I can never get it all right with my kids.

But what I can do is trust Him. I can live a life in surrender and dependence upon Him. Faith is turning to Him in realization of my inability, my lack of time, my insufficiency, my overbearing moments of putting my foot in my mouth, and my uncertain understanding of what the heck my kids need and when. Faith is asking for His involvement, activity, and resources.

I can't parent the way every book tells me to or the way every Pinterest post leads me. I can't possibly hit a home run every day. I don't have to. He wants to live His life through me. I'm not a bystander but a participant in the life of Jesus expressed and demonstrated in my life. I become a stage upon which He acts. He is the hand; I am the glove. My life is His choice to display His love and grace to the entire world—and to my own home.

I soaked up these freeing truths for myself. But why did I think this was only true for me as a mom?

There is a statement that floats around in my health coaching world: "Life is not happening *to* me but *for* me." Could it be, I reasoned, that the things my kids are experiencing are shaping *them* into incredible people? People who are resilient and kind because of the difficulties they've faced. People who are innovative and creative because of the limitations they've had to overcome. People who seek growth precisely because some stuff hasn't come easy.

The pressure valve releases as I guide my kids with this idea in mind. I don't become God in their lives. That job is way too big for me. And as it turns out, my kids aren't as tender and vulnerable as I thought. God is in control. God is their defense. God is the architect of their todays and tomorrows. And while my mom jobs are particularly important, God is managing His job perfectly.

On the road to true identity and intrinsic significance, we discover that life can be a bully. The world is unkind. There are some things we can do to improve as moms, but you're on the right path. You love your kids. You want to be a good mom that raises good humans and enjoys the journey of it all. But you are also imperfect. You have challenges and hard days just like everyone else. And though it may feel like you are running out of time to figure things out before it's too late and your kids are grown, let me assure you—*there's plenty of time.*

It's inevitable as parents that we will wound our children. Try as we might, we make mistakes. We sometimes fail to meet their needs because of our unmet needs from the past. We have blind spots and weaknesses and flaws that hurt those we love. But the beauty is that generational bondage can be broken when we get honest, name the pain, repent, and forgive. We cannot be wholehearted without owning our own wrongdoing. With a heart of radical responsibility, we can experience the fulfillment of so much of the promise, especially in our relational connections. Jesus is saying, "I'm glad you are here. There is no shame. Welcome to the party!"

We must recognize how we impact our kids because of our pain or fears. These are some things I've had to repent for:

* I'm sorry for the times I've controlled and dominated. I'm trying to help you avoid making my mistakes.
* I'm sorry for the times I'm quick-tempered that have caused you to withdraw.

* I'm sorry for overreacting to the information you share. It has breached your trust in our communication, which is essential for our relationship.

* I'm sorry for the times I've demanded your performance, resulting in your feelings of discouragement or inadequacy.

Identifying the places you have wounded or have been wounded is vital. We don't recall them to blame others or shame ourselves, but for healing. What is kept hidden cannot be healed. And what is not healed will be passed down to the generations to come. But if a curse can be passed down, so can a blessing. This is free living.

Charles Trumbull once said, "Jesus Christ does not want to be our helper; He wants to be our life. He does not want us to work for Him; He wants us to let Him do His work through us, using us as we use a pencil to write with—better still, using us as one of the fingers on His hand."

This does not mean our role as mom simply goes away. It doesn't mean we stop making decisions or being a powerful, shaping influence in our kids' lives. In fact, the moment we quit allowing mom guilt to bully us, and allow God to have control, we find ourselves more active and influential than ever before.

Letting go of control and embracing trust will cultivate a culture of grace. Grace for you and grace for others, including your kids.

"But just as you excel in everything—in faith, in speech, in knowledge, in complete earnestness and in your love for us—see that you also excel in this grace of giving." 2 Corinthians 8:7

What better way to live and to lead than by the value of grace? When controlling ceases, so does blame. And when we live our lives with a lot less mom guilt, bullying and self-condemnation, we begin to see the Lord working things out on our behalf.

"What is kept hidden cannot be healed."

23

GOING THROUGH HARD THINGS WITH KIDS

When we took the initial leap of starting the church, I understood the implications of the risk we were taking as adults. But additionally, a big factor of success for me was the state of my kids' well-being. I understood our choices would impact them, but I hoped it would be mostly easy and always good.

My kids were in preschool and early elementary, and I assumed their social resilience would make the transition to a new school easier. I could positively spin the sudden change in home size, and so I did. And like any good parent, we added a dog to the mix to make the move even more exciting.

But the one thing I could not manipulate with my words or deeds was the new role they would play as "Lead Pastor's kids." I knew they were too young to be burdened with many expectations from the congregation, but I worried about their future. Based on my tenure in church, I knew that the pressure on pastors' kids to be exemplary

Christians, always under the spotlight, frequently triggered issues. I had seen it happen in other ministry families in scary ways. So I prayed one prayer on repeat almost every day: "May my children love God's house and God's people."

God answered this prayer in spades. My kids were an active part of the church. They took pride in preparing the weekly kids' programs. They would help lead worship and put together the materials we would need for all the activities. They loved going early to set up and didn't mind tearing down. They enjoyed the people and became passionate about how we served the city.

One of their favorite things to do was pack up lunches after church in an assembly line with our congregation and head out in the neighborhood to feed our homeless friends. They were rarely afraid and often empowered. Their tiny hearts grasped the mission, and they were all in. Our faith community was good to them and gave them the best kind of attention. They experienced what it means to be seen, known, and loved. God heard my prayers, and He answered them.

But now we were leaving this church. We had a counselor guiding Marcus and me through the big transition, and we wanted our departure to be as uneventful as possible. But I knew telling our kids would be hard. Our counselor prepared us that it might be even more difficult than we expected.

To be honest, I downplayed the counselor's concern. We weren't moving. They wouldn't be changing schools. No one had died, and we weren't getting a divorce. But man, our counselor was right! We gathered the kids in our living room. It was a Friday night, and though they were used to huddling up for Jones Tribe talks, it was clear we had an agenda. We told our kids the news as concisely and honestly as possible without making it weird or over-spiritualized. We shared the facts and a few details about the change. And we attempted to wrap it all up with a pretty bow and this final statement: "God is moving us on.

We are going to obey. Sometimes obedience is painful, and we don't always understand. But it's going to be okay."

Then we asked if they had anything to say. Tears flowed down every one of their sweet, pre-adolescent faces. They were each hurting deeply in their own way, and I didn't imagine the profound ways each of them would articulate their emotions. It was the heart of my then twelve-year-old that caused me to panic. She began to share her thoughts, and I did not foresee it coming out this way. She said, "If God is good and has a plan, why would He do this to me? Why would He take away my most beloved place? Sundays are my favorite day of the week."

I sat speechless. I'd heard these similar words from many adults I'd mentored over the years, but hearing them from my eighth grader was next-level. They are the words spoken from a heart of deep sorrow. They are also words that often cause some to derail from their faith. I couldn't help but glance at my husband, the look in my eyes crying out silently for help. *Say something, Marcus. Make this better.*

"I don't know, sweet girl," is all we could muster.

There were moments in the weeks and months that followed when my mind went down crazy rabbit trails, worrying that the kids would be so traumatized by the grief from this loss that they would walk away from faith in God. Further spiraling, I would imagine them turning to drugs, alcohol, and promiscuous lifestyles to avert their pain. I know it's dramatic; but in the middle of watching my kids' anguish, these were the fears swirling inside my head. I had accepted that my obedience to God on this new journey would involve sacrifices, and I was willing to count the cost. But I wasn't so keen when it came to my kids counting the cost, too.

I set out to find a church home for our family after the departure from the one we had started. I created a list of the churches I was familiar with that had decent student ministries in our area. I also went online to research churches I didn't know as a gesture of openness to what God might provide as a solution to the problem we had created. My efforts felt noble, like something any good mom would do. My kids needed connection. They desired a church community. And I would fix it. If I didn't, then who would? And if I couldn't quickly, my kids might just lose their faith out in the streets.

At the moment, this fix-it attitude was my honest reaction that felt appropriate and good. But in hindsight, it was a flawed attempt to control. I was trying to manage my fears by supervising the outcomes, which only exacerbated them.

One day, a message notification popped up on my phone. It was from one of my husband's childhood friends, Amy. We had never met in person, but her family was always spoken of very fondly. After graduation, getting married, and having a few kids, Amy's parents left the country to be missionaries, choosing a path of challenge and sacrifice I was familiar with.

Amy described the good and the hard of her parents' choices. She shared that growing up, she both liked and disliked being a kid who lived in an impoverished country. She spoke of moments of resentment for being unable to have a normal life and be part of all the typical events and activities kids experience in the U.S.

And then she said something I desperately needed to hear. "But it made me who I am today." It was because of the obedience of her parents to follow Christ no matter the cost that she became a better human with a very fulfilling life. She didn't deny that it was challenging at times, but it was the hard that produced the good. She attributed her heart for people, her passion for God, how she raises her children, and how she leads in her career to her upbringing on the mission field. Then she made one last statement that penetrated the deepest part of my heart. She wrote, "If it's God's plan for you, then it's God's plan for your kids."

Like Amy's parents, God was clearly unconventionally leading my family, and I was afraid of the impact on my kids. Amy's statement gave me a new perspective. My responsibility to obey God was bigger than me. It was also shaping my children. Who was I to believe I knew better and could craft the right steps for the future of each of my kids?

I was challenged to confront my fears, release control, and obey the Lord on behalf of my babies. I didn't want to rob them of these God-led experiences that were part of the story He was writing in them.

We often disqualify a decision because we fear it might make life harder for our kids, as if we can control every negative risk and turn it into a positive outcome. We know deep down we can't deliver on that power, but we often live in the delusion we are in more control than we actually are. Through my personal experiences in this area, I've learned I have to prepare my child for the path, not the path for my child.

> *"If it's God's plan for you, then it's God's plan for your kids."*

This challenged my assumption that God wouldn't ask me to do something that put our kids at risk. *Life is risky.* It's tumultuous and can be hard. Part of parenting is fully surrendering our families, knowing He loves our children even more than we do. Ultimately, the parenting mission is not to shelter our children in fear, but to send them out in love.

No matter what season of parenting you find yourself in or what God is asking of you—you can quickly find fear. In fact, it finds you. The world is dangerous, scary, and unpredictable. But we cannot put our kids in a bubble or shelter them from the world because of our fears. Parents never lack things to worry about. God knows your fears, and He is greater than them all.

"Ultimately, the parenting mission is not to shelter our children in fear, but to send them out in love."

"Cast all your anxiety on him because he cares for you." 1 Peter 5:7

Before God entrusted our kids to us, He knew what they would need and deemed us fit to help provide for them. No matter how big or small your fear might be, behind those thoughts is the worry that you may not be "doing it right." That somehow, you're messing them up and that your mistakes as a parent will hinder God's purpose for their lives. *This is a lie.* And one I sometimes bought into.

During those times, I would cling tightly to Amy's words, coupled with this promise in Psalm 119, "Your faithfulness endures to every generation; You founded the earth, and it remains."

This is a prevailing promise of God. I cannot protect my kids from discomfort; I would pay them a disservice if I did. As hard as it is for me to stand by and watch, I cannot protect them from change or challenge.

This process of growing through hardship—of accepting the path that's paved with suffering and is as painful as you expected—is the only way to move from anxiety to trust. It can be a tough thing. Sometimes the hard thing and the right thing are the same thing.

In all my years of living, I can say confidently that every good thing I have ever attained has presented itself through the hard. Furthermore, the hard thing consistently propels me to a new level in my faith and life. This is true for you and me as parents. The same is true for our kids.

If we desire for our children to live free and truly alive, we must bring them with us into hard things. That cannot happen when we are locked up in worry, over-protecting every step they take. Let's ignore the voice of fear and no longer listen to that accusing whisper. Let's not parent out of panic of what might happen or who our children might become, but let's flip the script and parent by faith in who God desires them to be.

As my children have grown older, they are charged with making more decisions on their own. And even when they might be better served if they consulted us, often they don't. It's difficult to watch as some of their choices lead them to growth through hard lessons. But this is when we must trust the Holy Spirit. Hidden patterns are embedded in our experiences that point to God's divine direction and ultimate intention for us and our kids' lives.

God created each of us with gifts, insights, and abilities. We are all designed with unique personalities and a natural bent that reveals His plan along the way. When God makes a map, it is a masterpiece. So, trust His path.

24

TOES UNDER THE TABLE

Our family is affectionately referred to as "the Jones Tribe." We gave ourselves this name and have grown very fond of it. We have values in our Tribe, as every family does. We've just written ours down and prominently displayed them in our living room. We're all about making sure what matters most doesn't just mull around in the back of someone's mind. But that's it's forward and loud and lived-out.

One of our favorite values is that we do "toes under the table", meaning that we consistently gather for a decent dinner together. Every toe in the Tribe is under the same table. I don't expect that this will happen every night at this stage of our family game, but I will settle for three nights a week. Sometimes I'm lucky enough to get four (Sunday lunch out after church counts).

This habit is not about the food, and I'm certainly not polishing up the place-settings (I'm a big believer in paper plates). It's about *the gathering*. It's about creating the space for our forever community. Studies show that when community and connection happen in a family dynamic, it contributes to a person's identity, their sense of self and their self-esteem greatly benefits. That's my goal.

Another one of our values is Legacy. Our family is our lasting heritage: the lives we touch, the memories we make, and the smiles we bring to the face of God and one another. That's our legacy. While it is my great desire to impact the world, I want to be most influential in my own home. So, a commitment to "toes under the table" it is.

> *Starting meaningful conversations within our families isn't always easy.*

Now before you start imagining some Pleasantville-type scenario, remember that many nights it's all happening on paper plates. I'm not wearing an apron and Marcus isn't sitting at the head of the table like a castle lord. We're just gathered. It's not even always at the same time each week due to sports practices and late night activities. This often will lead to some grumbling and complaining from another kid because they are starving, and we are waiting for the sibling who is arriving late. It's rarely ideal, but it always matters.

Starting meaningful conversations within our families isn't always easy. We want to connect with them and build positive relationships, but it can be challenging at times. It sounds cliche, but things just aren't the way they used to be. When I was young, we didn't have smartphones; social media wasn't a thing. But our kids' generation is exposed to an entire world in the palm of their hands, which has its upsides, but also leads to a lot of pressure. It's difficult for me to fully understand their experience, which makes communication a challenge.

What is similar for both of our generations is that being a teen is filled with many ups and downs. Our children experience pressure and need support from their parents. In order to help them, we need to gain their trust by starting authentic conversations and spending time getting to know their needs and interests. Because of this, my goal is to get my kids talking. So our round table discussions rarely start with yes or no questions. We keep things open-ended. When my kids do start talking, I've learned that my best response is not to be surprised, shocked, disappointed, or to overreact. I do a lot of listening and way less talking, even though I do have a lot to say. I lecture less and listen more.

Deliberately deciding to listen—staying focused on the speaker without interjecting our own ideas and solutions—is powerful. Asking questions instead of giving answers enables a safe space for everyone to share. Trying to see the world from where our kids sit (even if it's irrational or irrelevant) is sometimes hard. Controlling my impulse to speak sometimes has me biting my tongue (literally). But validating emotions and listening to what they think is a good idea and worth it.

Asking good questions is almost a lost art these days. And we parents can fall into the trap of believing we're supposed to have an answer for every problem. When we become preoccupied with shelling out answers, we short-circuit our ability to soothe emotions and see the heart of the matter. Asking questions is challenging sometimes. But the connections they draw are priceless.

I'm often uncomfortable during these conversations. My kids don't make me uncomfortable. But feeling out of full control certainly does. And questions are about curiosity, not control. We have incredible influence over our kids. But influence is a privilege, not an entitlement.

According to Philippians 3:21, only God has "power that enables everything under his control." I choose to submit to the authority of Christ by bringing all things, including my parenting, to Him. I have decided to join Him in the work He is doing in my children. Surrender brings discomfort. *Often.* It goes against the grain of my will, but yielding power over my children's life is the only way to gain the influence I desperately desire, and we all need.

It's been fascinating to watch the sixteen-year-old in me rise up on occasion when dealing with my own teenagers. Sometimes I receive my kids' lack of reasoning or emotional tendencies as a personal affront. It's not, of course, but outbursts still occur.

I have to remind myself that I am a full grown adult; and as tempting as it might be to indulge my late-stage adolescence, I need to surrender my need to always be right. Wisdom in parenting often means taking a deep breath and apologizing. I say I'm sorry (a lot). My offense may not always be severe, but modeling humility and saying sorry creates an environment of repentance and forgiveness. Great tribes intentionally cultivate a culture willing to say "I'm sorry" and "I forgive you".

It's fair to say that I'm still practicing with all of this. In a recent table talk, one of my daughters brought up her ideas about college. She is getting to the stage where she needs to start seriously looking at where she might want to attend. As she began to describe the environment she desired and the activities she wanted to participate in, I recognized that she wanted to go somewhere far from home. The only thing that might keep her tied to her home state was the ocean, but she was open to considering the other coast.

Listening to her, my heart sank. She is very capable and quite independent, like her mother; and I want her to soar. But...*why?* Why did she want to go so far away? Was it to get away from us? I could feel the fear creeping up on me, but I fought the urge to overreact and gently said, "Tell me more about that." I think my tone gave away what I was really asking (*"Will you even miss us?!"*) because her immediate response was, "I don't want to get away from you guys! Of course, I'll miss everyone. I just want to go explore and take on adventures. I know I can always come home."

"Great tribes intentionally cultivate a culture willing to say 'I'm sorry' and 'I forgive you'."

In today's world, I can track my kids on their smartphones, and we are literally never technically detached. This has caused parents to relate to kids in a way that essentially prolongs childhood. I will admit that I personally had to make a shift in my thinking and release the leash. Instead of fostering or promoting reliance among my kids by wanting them to always stay close, prolonging their childhood, I focus my efforts on creating an unconditionally loving space that is connected through vulnerability and safety so that they would be empowered to go create their own life.

Toes under the table is really my way of preparing them to become happy and successful young adults. Toes under the table is one of the ways I create a place for them to be fully known. Toes under the table is a foundation-creating moment to help my kids have their feet firmly planted, so they can go reach for the stars.

My daughter's desire to go away to college is a result of the community we have built at home. She has a foundation that propels her forward instead of holding her back. The Tribe is her launching pad, not her handcuffs. Because let's face it, her desire is healthy and natural. This longing for adventure is not because she wants to leave the strong community we built with our Tribe, but *because* of it. Raising teenagers especially is constantly sitting at the crossroads of wanting to hang on tight, keeping them safe within your grasp, and letting them go to figure out this life and all its hard stuff on their own.

This is not for the faint of heart. It's an invitation to the courageous. Consider the gift you can give to your kids. Building a Tribe that is rooted, solid, and passionate about belonging delivers confidence, strength, and capacity to take on their life's journey in a way that is divinely different.

25

MAKING FRIENDS

At one point during our crazy journey, my four kids were at three different schools. Jumping into new environments, breaking the ice, and connecting with others can be tough; and I was most anxious about their social life. Interestingly, bopping from school to school thrust me into the same challenge.

I remember volunteering to chaperone on a sixth-grade field trip. Oddly, being surrounded by a bunch of eleven-year-olds wasn't the biggest challenge. It was being encircled by a bunch of moms I didn't know that created the most apprehension for me. Would I take the advice I so often dished out to my kids about putting themselves out there to connect? Or would I shrink back—hiding behind my duty as guardian—and stick to myself?

Funny how much junior high fear and awkwardness still kicks around inside a mature woman in her forties. *What would these moms think of me? Would they like me? Would they want to be my friends?*

I asked this question with trepidation. Like many, I have friendship baggage. In my 20's, I was busy acquiring as many friends as possible.

To balance the angst of trying to "figure out" my future, I filled my life with more people and more fun.

In my 30's, the friends from my twenties began to thin out. I settled in, married my man, began to have babies, and built our home. My time and treasure shifted, which left some friendships on the outs.

During these decades, I didn't always have a healthy view of friendship. I sometimes held onto fantasies about what others could be in my life rather than what they actually were. My dysfunction led me to play the hero, holding on too tightly and sometimes pushing people away. As a result, my friendship story often went like this: "It's not you, it's me." This line, filled with rejection, had me frequently feeling like something must be wrong with me. As a result, I walked away a little more alone each time I heard it.

> *Wanting to belong is a fundamental human need.*

Now I sit in my 40's having done the deeper work of truly knowing who I am. I better understand the depths of God's love for me, and the source of my true identity. I have become more aware of the things that drive me and the kind of people who fuel me. In this process, I have lost a few friendships. For the longest time, I thought that was my fault, but now I realize that maybe something was right. This is the decade when my friendships may be fewer, but they run deep.

Wanting to belong is a fundamental human need. If it was unimportant, we would live solitary lives. We would have no families, communities or organized government.

We cannot separate the importance of a sense of belonging from our physical and mental health. The social ties that accompany a sense of belonging are key components to our ability to manage stress and curb negative behavioral patterns. When we feel we have support and are not alone, we are more resilient, coping more effectively with difficult times in our lives. Coping well with hardships decreases the physical and mental effects of these situations. Belonging, community, and the connection to others really is a habit of health.

The beginning of our fundamental need for belonging starts in our families. Children who have not achieved a healthy attachment in their young life have less confidence, a more negative worldview, are mistrustful, and struggle with rejection. Conversely, the desire to go out and brave the world in adventure can be attributed to healthy attachment.

Whether we experienced belonging young, or are late to the party creating it, the good news is that we have the power to make changes in our lives to bolster our sense of belonging.

The most crucial ingredient to building a sense of belonging is effort. You cannot belong if you don't choose to make the effort to engage with others. It may feel uncomfortable at first to meet new people, but give it time. Soon the actions will become second nature because right feelings follow right actions.

Back to my chaperone story. There I was, with all my friendship baggage, waffling about what to do. Quickly I realized that waiting for someone to make friendship happen for me wasn't going to happen. I decided to take my own advice and push out of my comfort zone.

I'm not sure there is any way to skip past the heart work of creating friendship. No real way to avoid the pain to receive the joy. No shortcuts to developing rich relationships—in fact the more you grow, the more they go. But take it from me—it's worth the work. Don't settle. You will find the ones convinced of your worth. Lock arms with those ones. Together you will soar, and it will be so much fun.

It starts with practice. It sounds simple and even a little silly to say but say, "Hi" first. How often are we resistant to utter this first word?

As you stand awkwardly side by side, you can either scroll through your phone to avoid eye contact, or you can suck it up and say it. Simply smile, act excited about what you are doing and say, "Hello." It didn't kill me, and it won't kill you.

What happens after "Hello"? It's quite possible you get what you dread: awkward silence. Just press past it and begin. It likely won't start with deep conversation. But connecting on common interests or even the weather will work. Even if you aren't the kind of person who finds it easy to strike up a conversation with a total stranger, the alternative is uncomfortable silence for hours on a field trip.

A key to this kind of connection is to be interested. As I cracked open the conversation with a safe topic or two, I discovered some new information about the other moms. That's when I decided to take the risk and ask something more personal. I was gentle and careful. But genuine interest led to some cool chat.

It's important to stay positive when you're just breaking the ice. While we did get into some mom hot topics, I kept it neutral. It was clear we wouldn't agree on all things, so I guided the conversation toward things we had in common. Building community requires cultivating trust and that takes time.

In this process of creating community, it's important to always be you. Your world needs who *you* are, not a faux version of somebody else. God has placed you on this path and is intersecting your life with people. On the field trip that day, a small part of me felt like I had been time warped back to middle school. I had to remind myself: "You're not thirteen anymore, Jen. You're a grown woman. Hold your head up and be you."

Reject the tendency to posture or pretend, or even say what you think they may want to hear. Be yourself. Ultimately, people like you for you. So, forget being artificial. Ditch the urge to come off in some contrived way. Just be you.

"People will forget what you said, people will forget what you did, but people will never forget how you made them feel."
Maya Angelou

Summer leaves me with these warm feelings. Not just because the sun is out. Where I live in San Diego, it's always 74 degrees and sunny. It's more about the season of the year. Each season of the year has its charm. But for me, summer is all about "connection." It's not a time to hustle big dreams and goals. It's become a time that I enjoy the fruit of spring and get ready for a fall harvest. In summer, I sit, I play, I commune with friends, and break bread. Well, not literally bread because most of my friends and I don't eat much of that. But you get the picture.

During one particular summer, I found myself setting a table for eight to gather my friends together. It was "toes under the table," only with friends instead of family. The night started with laughter—and lots of it. It was a night to celebrate the past and hope for our futures. As we sat to enjoy the tossed greens in zesty vinaigrette, the salmon baked lightly in a dill aioli sauce, and the roasted veggies seasoned to perfection, one of the girls said a prayer. It was more of a proclamation: *God, this is what I see: I see Kingdom women. Each one has so much to give, and each one benefits the other.*

Amen, right? Throughout the years, this table of eight has met repeatedly. Together we have endured change. We have processed pain together. We grieved for a loss. We struggled through infertility side-by-side and believed for new life. We battled depression and overcame guilt from past shame. We fought and conquered addictions, and together we embraced grace. We prayed for our children and shared the load of building one another's dreams. We called it Supper Club.

At Supper Club, we are not alike, but we champion our differences. Every successful community I've created or joined has had a common thread of shared values. This doesn't mean everyone believes exactly the same way or has the same perspective on every issue or situation. Even so, shared values make for true connection and meaningful conversations. There is a benefit to the table being filled with elements of diversity to create space for everyone to learn and to grow. This is a Biblical framework for true community as written in Proverbs 27:17:

"As iron sharpens iron, so one person sharpens another."

No one goes it alone. And to make yourself better, there is an incredible benefit to leaning into mentorship, leadership, friendship, and community. We believe the best and hope for better. Together we build confidence. Together we live out a transformational truth: if you're not changing, you're not growing.

Change is hard. Most of us avoid it at any cost. I know I have tried. But avoiding change creates even bigger problems, like lost opportunities, broken relationships, and sometimes even wasted potential. Isolation can exacerbate these problems; but in the community, we are reminded that in this world, we will have trouble. And that trouble can work for our good. These lessons are much easier to walk out in the circle of trust, knowing we truly are stronger together.

"Though one may be overpowered, two can defend themselves. A cord of three strands is not quickly broken." Ecclesiastes 4:12

We are going to be thrown curveballs in this life. Hard things will happen. The unknown is scary, but don't be afraid. When there is buy in from all the toes under the table, a supper club can change your life. Maybe it's time to create your own table of eight. Around this meaningful meal, amidst the breaking of bread, each one has something valuable to give and something precious to gain.

26

HEALING AND RECONCILIATION

I cannot talk about this topic of community without addressing the reality that this is the primary place many of us have been hurt. I've spent my entire life in church. My best friends came from the church. And some of my greatest heartaches have come from that same place. I've hurt church girls and church girls have hurt me. So a few years ago, when I walked into a church by choice instead of assignment, I was definitely coming in guarded and seriously scoping things out.

And this is what I quickly learned: when there are broken relationships in your past, God will use new relationships to heal those wounds. God will use relationships to heal your heart, if that's what you want. And the connection will propel you forward because God created us for each other. Even if we're a little guarded, God honors the obedience.

Community heals, even if it hurts first. What's broken in relationship is healed in relationship. I've experienced cattiness and competitiveness in communities I trusted. And that hurt. But I've also experienced the healing salve of friends who believed the best in me and selflessly gave of themselves so I could win.

"When there are broken relationships in your past, God will use new relationships to heal those wounds."

I've been betrayed and abandoned in relationships. And I have the scars to prove it. But I've also experienced the mending power that friendship can bring in response to that trauma. I've known loyalty and faithfulness. I've been on the receiving end of steadfast love.

If you can relate to the sting that comes from relational pain, you can probably relate to the temptation to be guarded when you walk into new circles. First time, shame on you. Second time, shame on me, right? But unfortunately, time doesn't actually heal all hurts. Usually, hurt must be tended to. Brokenness needs mending. And the cure for what has wounded you in failed friendships is actually found in healthy ones.

Our hurt can separate us from the very thing that will bring us healing. I am actually in awe at the divinity of Jesus and His care for our meaningful connection. Be open to who God might bring to you.

It can be easy to create your safety zone—an us-four-no-more mentality. Some of the fullest friendships I have came at an unlikely time or in an improbable way. Had I been closed off, or disobedient to God's promptings, I would have missed out on faithful friendships that have been like medicine to my life.

Jump into the joy God can bring to you through the people He has put in your path. What it looked like for me was sharing my struggles, weaknesses, and fears with caring friends, who were able to listen and go to God with me for help and mercy. Through this process I became whole. It will still require you to take a chance, but you will discover that you are not alone. Community restores.

"By wisdom a house is built, and through understanding it is established." Proverbs 24:3

I think it's safe to say we all want to build a solid life. The passage above in Proverbs 24 makes it clear that establishing the life you want to live requires understanding. Our community is full of people. Anytime people are around, you can expect to encounter lots of *mis*understandings.

So how do we have the abundant life God promises us when often the relationships in our life experience conflict? It's important to realize that while God promises life that is blessed beyond measure, it doesn't mean it will be perfect and without problems. The New Testament describes a rich relationship with Jesus and others as equivalent to sharing in sufferings.

Shallow friends do the easy stuff. Dear friends are there when life gets messy. True community, there through the highs and lows, requires the comprehension and faithful application of 2 Corinthians 5:18-19:

> *"All this is from God, who reconciled us to himself through Christ and gave us the ministry of reconciliation: that God was reconciling the world to himself in Christ, not counting people's sins against them. And he has committed to us the message of reconciliation."*

To break it down: reconciliation is what God is doing here on Earth. He is drawing people back to Himself. Furthermore, He is charging us to spread love. Reconciliation is like a bridge to a reunion between you and me. Without it, we are separated and broken. With it, we are connected and healed. When we aren't good with one another, God isn't good with it either.

I've had to walk out this kind of reconciliation myself with my sister-in-law, Lindsey. Although we are often mistaken as blood sisters, we are in-laws. She married my brother. We both love God, love our families, have similar interests and by all appearances would seem perfectly cool with each other. But things haven't always been as they've seemed.

In the first decade of our life as sisters-in-law, we sometimes collided. There have been times that we've created tension in our family relationships. There came one moment in time when we decided it was make it or break it. Considering the entire family wanted a positive outcome, you might assume reconciliation was easy. But years of mutual differences and offenses left both of us with built up hurts and piled-on misunderstandings.

Relational division happens in our lives. There is no way around it. Hebrews 12:15 says, "See to it that no one falls short of the grace of God and that no bitter root grows up to cause trouble and defile many."

This means that your offender is loved by God and is a recipient of His grace, just like you. Yes, you feel pain if you've been wronged. It hurts. But there is a bigger picture that reveals God is at work, even in our pain. And it's not all about you. In fact, how you handle disagreement can either compel others toward Christ or fatally taint their picture of Him.

> *Cast your cares on God. He will sustain you.*

So be careful. Don't get bitter. Be aware that conflict is inevitable and can be the beginning of a stronger relationship in the end.

"Humble yourselves, therefore, under God's mighty hand, that he may lift you up in due time." 1 Peter 5:6

Whether you're the offender or the offended, you can never go wrong when you go low. Don't fight for yourself. Humble yourself. If you need to be exonerated, God should be the one doing the job. Pray an honest prayer; acknowledge your hurts. Then ask God for the courage to communicate the truth in love. Cast your cares on God. He will sustain you.

Then repent. We must own our part in the community conflict. What's my part to play here? Am I being the friend I hope to have? Conviction isn't God calling you *out*. It's God calling you *up* to a higher way of living. Walking this out means confronting the one you are at odds with. You must do this with the goal of restoring the relationship, not winning the argument. This is hard. It's counter to our way of thinking much of the time. But it's in complete alignment with God's standards, which always results in abundant living.

Ephesians 4:15-16 says, "Speaking the truth in love, we will grow to become in every respect the mature body of him who is the head, that is, Christ. From him the whole body, joined and held together by every supporting ligament, grows and builds itself up in love, as each part does its work."

Remember, there's a bigger picture. It's not all about you. You and I have been called to reconciliation. And we all grow when the ultimate goal is restoration. Lindsey and I deliberately walked through this process. The result was a genuine and healthy change in our relationship. The outcome of our conflict, when worked through God's way, resulted in a powerful strengthening of our relationship. In the end, it was all good. It didn't mean bad never occurred again in our relationship. But Lindsey and I are deeply connected and have a solid foundation to navigate life's inevitable challenges better than ever. Today, we are more than in-laws. We are sisters. And we are friends.

27

IT'S NEVER TOO LATE TO FIND COMMUNITY

I had a conversation with a good friend about loving and leading people. "It just requires tough skin and a soft heart," I said. She replied with this great quote from Brené Brown, "Strong back, soft front, wild heart."

People are the source of so much joy and inspiration for me. I think they can be for you, too. We often walk around brittle and defensive, trying to conceal our fear of rejection or conceal our lack of confidence. But if we strengthen our backs, metaphorically speaking, and develop a spine that's flexible but sturdy, then we can risk having a front that's soft and open.

Perhaps if we all let down our guard, honestly confessing our desire for friends mixed with hesitation because of other failed attempts or burned bridges, a true community could be created; and friendships would represent less hurt and more healing.

The cross is history's most heroic act of friendship. Jesus wants us to view the cross in terms of friendship. On the night before He died, as He explained the meaning of the cross to His disciples, Jesus said in John 15:13, "Greater love has no one than this, that someone lay down his life for his friends."

The cross is certainly where Jesus bore the wrath of God in our place. But it is also, very personally, a relational act of sacrificial friendship. Through His death, Jesus expressed the deepest love for His people. He did not die for a nameless, faceless humanity; He died for specific people—real names, real lives, real hearts. He died for those He yearned to be His dear friends. He died for you, and He died for me.

One of my greatest discoveries in community is its power to cultivate courage. There is no reason that the coming together has to remain at the dinner table. It's a great place to start, but the possibilities are endless. Some of my richest relationships were forged with my feet on the soil of a mission field. Community has been created on the sidewalks of my city, serving lunches to those with no home.

When you invest yourself into life-giving community, you will find the courage you need to fulfill your call. The power you find in a circle of friends can move you toward the next great step God has for you.

The primary goal as a Christ-follower is to be more like Jesus. Following Him—being changed by Him—is called discipleship. Community is a key element in discipleship. When Jesus called His disciples, He called them to relationship: a community where they would do life together side by side. The call to this Christian life is often uncomfortable, but it is never wrong. It may be hard, but it will be best. And God uses community to shape us and use us for His kingdom.

Allow community to give you the courage to reach beyond yourself. You will learn to love. This is the second greatest command: to love your neighbor as yourself. Love cannot be done in seclusion. In community, you will be stretched to love imperfect people. Jesus spent most of His time with a somewhat motley crew of everyday people, and so should we.

Denying myself to love another person has transformed me into the likeness of Christ. And that is ultimately what this journey of life is all about.

Let community propel you forward.

We find bravery to move forward when we invest ourselves in community. It is there that we find support to pursue dreams, follow gut instincts, and obey promptings we've been sensing from the Holy Spirit. Matthew 18:20 says, "For where two or three gather in my name, there am I with them." When a community gathers in Jesus' name, Jesus always shows up.

In a small group of gals, I have watched my friends take their next right step in water baptism. For some, the act of this very public profession of faith is daunting. But when surrounded by a group of safe friends, it not only becomes doable, it is also foundational.

> *Let community propel you forward.*

Many have received courage to grow their families: some through natural conception and others through the gift of adoption and foster care. When surrounded by the faith of dear friends, many fears are put to rest.

As a community, we have served our city by feeding homeless people and giving gifts and clothing to those in need. We have invested time and effort cleaning and organizing shelters, childcare centers and other non-profits for the hurting and abused. Alone, we would have been only a drop in the bucket. But together—in community—we made a splash.

The first problem in the world was not of sin but of solitude. Each step of the way when God created the world, He pronounced that everything was good. But once he created Adam, a different statement was made: something is not good. And sin hadn't even showed up yet.

"It is not good for the man to be alone." Genesis 2:18

Interesting, isn't it? Sin hadn't even entered the world yet, and God's identifying a problem. Adam was not yet complete; he needed community. He needed a partner. A friend.

Friendship shows the world that we belong to Jesus. When this lonely world of broken relationships sees people of faith surrounded with friendships—imperfect friendships, to be sure, but relationships filled with true repentance and forgiveness—then they will know that something has come from above. They will see that our talk of Jesus is real.

"By this everyone will know that you are my disciples, if you love one another." John 13:35

So, start where you are. Who is in your world currently that you want to befriend? It doesn't matter if you have ten people you can think of or just one. We are only responsible to steward what is in our hands. Handle with care your current relationships, or the new one just around the corner, and I promise God will fill your life with more. I give you permission for it to look differently than past friendships or even connections you've had in your family. There is no one-size-fits-all in community relations. Just don't sit on the sidelines waiting for it to come to you. In a world full of 'look at me' people, join me; and together let's be 'come with me' people.

28

TRUE INFLUENCE

When I was a kid, I wanted to be a household name. No joke. I told my mom at the ripe old age of eight. Popularity was important to me, and the lifelong approval of man has been my plight. As it turns out, eight-year-old me would have fit in just fine today.

We live in a world where the word "influencer" is now a job. Ask a young Gen Z kid what they want to do for a living and "influencer" tops the list of responses. A recent study indicated that out of 1,000 kids surveyed in the US, 29 percent wanted to become YouTube stars.[5] In fact, as I was doing the research for these statistics, one of the top titles in my search was, "How do I make my child a YouTube star?"

In our social media society, an influencer is defined as someone who has a lot of followers on their YouTube, Snapchat, or Instagram accounts. They are likely attractive with some unique ability and promote products. Regardless of the cost or credibility of the product,

---

[5] Dzhanova, Yelena. "Forget Law School, These Kids Want to Be a YouTube Star." CNBC, CNBC, 3 Aug. 2019, https://www.cnbc.com/2019/08/02/forget-law-school-these-kids-want-to-be-a-youtube-star.html.

their popularity makes it an immediate must-have. They aren't more educated or more skilled or even more capable than the rest. They aren't happier or more satisfied. They haven't discovered the true meaning of life. They just found their niche on social media and a lot of people have decided to watch. These influencers are often young, unfiltered, and bold enough to live their life loudly and online.

Another study answered the question "Why?" Why do kids want to be an "influencer" over being an astronaut? The short answer: identity.

Not only are YouTubers on par with conventional celebrities, but they are seen as powerful and influential icons. Becoming a YouTuber is now one of the most popular career choices for children. Being on the social stage is seen as important. It makes them feel worthy, and it gives them a sense of community by numbers of likes and follows.

The social stage is sought after by more than 50 percent of Millennials and Generation Z who are determined to create content and get paid for it.[6] I don't judge this pursuit; in my own Generation-X-way, I have had the same desires. We all do. The need for our lives to matter is innate. According to Abraham Maslow in his famous paper "A Theory of Human Motivation" and more fully in his book *Motivation and Personality*, we all follow a universal hierarchy of human needs. Our base needs are survival necessities such as food, water and sleep, but the top of the triangle is a desire to achieve and make a difference. In modern society this often translates to recognition and influence. What Maslow does not include in his theory is our need for God, which we need more than anything and is what motivates all our attempts to achieve true wholeness. Maslow, for all his insights, failed to recognize the God who created the entire triangle.

---

[6] Jennings, Rebecca. "*So Your Kid Wants to Be an Influencer.*" Vox, Vox, 31 Aug. 2022, https://www.vox.com/the-goods/2022/8/31/23328677/kid-influencer-ryans-world-ellie-zeiler.

The definition of influence is: the capacity to have an effect on the character, development, or behavior of someone or something, or the effect itself. By definition, influence is not numeric. In a world based on numbers like follows and likes, this truth about influence brought relief to my soul. Not only for me but for the generations to come.

Influence is about transformation. True transformation is when genuine connection is made in a relationship. Your influence may impact ten thousand, but it is already fulfilled when you've influenced one. Once God helped me to change the way I viewed influence, it freed me up to own the way I actually do make an impact.

We all have been given something to do. For some that will mean influence in a contemporary, "social media" sense. There are tremendous upsides to having a virtual microphone and using it for good.

There will always be incredible impacts that can be made on a platform for a large audience. The trouble I see is that too many of us want to be famous, not effective. More than a few of us want influence before we've done anything to earn it. And even then, influence in and of itself *isn't* a worthy goal and never should be. Being an effective, humble influencer who helps the people you're assigned to is the goal.

Without a doubt, we live in a celebrity culture. It's interesting that we can be fascinated with people we'll never meet and who likely have little desire to meet us. But we are. And in the last decade, celebrity culture has taken hold in our lives. It can consume our hearts and minds, sucking up our time. At times we've become more interested in the details of the lives of celebrity leaders than our own lives and those we get to serve.

While it is easy to blame technology, we must always go back to taking radical responsibility if we want to find freedom and live a significant life. Technology isn't good or evil; it just reveals and amplifies what's already there. Paul and the early church struggled with this

"True transformation
is when
genuine connection
is made in a
relationship."

issue almost 2000 years before anyone even thought of smartphones or Instagram. The problem isn't necessarily new. It's just amplified.

I recognize that having fans and popularity feels good at a certain level; but as we encounter Jesus and are transformed by His grace, we discover a significance no human could ever author. The foundation of our faith is built on the person and work of Jesus, not our popularity, success, nor the promises of the American dream.

The ambition of the cross and the modern world's views on influence simply cannot go hand in hand; they are majorly at odds and hopelessly incompatible. Christ, accepting the cross in all of its shame and weakness, turned the offer of worldly influence with all its appeal and glamor on its ear.

My plea as a young child was to be famous. But it was my mom who cried out to God that there be favor, not fame, on my life. God heard her heart, and the journey to life change and Biblical perspective has been the path of

> *Being an influencer is not an identity.*

my life. For a long time, I craved the influence and the spotlight because it fed my need for approval and significance. But after experiencing the freedom that came from no longer attaching my value to achievements, I began to realize how limited and temporary that spotlight can be.

Events in the spotlight are just moments in time; they can be fun, but they do not deliver true meaning. Being an influencer is not an identity.

God has given all of us something to do. For some that might mean celebrity influence. But your identity is not in what produces the eyeballs, likes, follows, or dollars for your life. When we can lay down our need to influence at the feet of Jesus in surrender, we become open to experience true significance.

The difference between success and significance is leveraging your influence for others who may have nothing and can give you nothing. When the blessing of influence is only for us, it is wasted. This shift in thinking will put an end to leaders, influencers, and entrepreneurs who are striving to grow their own kingdoms; and it will be the beginning of leaders who will start growing His.

At the end of Mother Teresa's 1984 Nobel Prize acceptance speech she said, "And so, my prayer for you is that truth will bring prayer in our homes, and from the foot of prayer will be that we believe that in the poor it is Christ. And we will really believe, we will begin to love. And we will love naturally, we will try to do something. First in our own home, next door neighbor, in the country we live, in the whole world."

From this speech has derived a more commonly quoted saying that goes, "If you want to change the whole world, go home and love your family."

This idea—that influence can be huge when it's also very small—helped me see the vastness of my influence when I live my life with intent to love the ones in front of me, instead of chasing after the ones who may never even know my name. I am a true influencer when I sit toes under the table at home, sharing stories with my husband and children and playing my part in their life, connecting at an intimate level. This conversation, this level of care, changes the narrative in their lives. In response, they own their story, which will reach beyond our four walls to the world, where even more change occurs.

I am not suggesting that I don't want to use my gifts in a way that communicates the health and hope of Jesus to a large audience. The spotlight comes somewhat naturally to me. I desire to serve the world, and that often occurs through the multiplication process of broadening my reach on a magnified platform.

However, there is something powerful about being with people. Sitting and holding space across a coffee table with two or three creates the significance we crave. Small circles, not big stages, create the kind of influence we all truly need.

29

CELEBRATING CIRCLES

Every Monday morning, I gather on a Zoom call with women from all over the country. Two things we have in common: we love Jesus, and we are building our health coaching business together. Make it three things: we all desire to grow.

One of these Mondays, God interrupted our conversation. Before I began, I felt the tug in my heart to talk less and listen more. Someone needed to be seen that morning and obedience always wins the day. Which is exactly what the first girl to share had to say.

The Lord had called her out of comfort, wealth, nice things, easy money, and the security she had known for a few years, and into *trust*. The 'all in' kind of faith that requires selling your things and giving up ease. The kind of dependence that has a path but isn't sure exactly where it will lead and what exactly it will provide. The kind of belief that says no matter what, I will follow.

"The Lord gives and the Lord takes away. Blessed be the name of the Lord." Job 1:21 CSB

As she shared, tears rolled down my cheeks. These are the girls that I want to be surrounded by. The kind of girls who pursue the abundance of Jesus, knowing full well His kind of wealth does not necessarily equal material things. Jesus first. Always.

"So above all, constantly seek God's kingdom and his righteousness, then all these less important things will be given to you abundantly." Matthew 6:33 TPT

I believe it is in these circles that the Holy Spirit readily reveals Himself. We experience the comfort of God in our pain—together. We are encouraged in our faith by the testimony of others. And we can believe for the greater promises He has for our lives because we are not alone. My life has been shaped by circles like this.

I grew up as a Christian girl. It was then, within a small circle of girls named "Missionettes," led by a woman of faith, that my foundation of faith was forged. This first layer of my early childhood discipleship helped me make good choices through the school years. I felt I was on a mission to be salt and light, spreading hope by inviting my friends to church.

As I approached college, my circle got smaller, and I began to struggle. This was the season I felt a little lost and my decisions reflected this fact. I found myself floundering a bit and making decisions that were not true to my core. I can now see that I was feeling a loss of identity in early adulthood and was very uncertain about where I fit. The wandering ultimately led me back to God, leading me back for mercy, forgiveness, and help.

This is when I discovered the next circle that quite literally reshaped the trajectory of my life. This circle was a choice to move from the comfort of sunny San Diego to an unfamiliar, blazing hot Arizona. Here, in this space with a small group of zealous twenty-somethings that loved the Lord, we made a splash for God's Kingdom. We traveled as missionaries both locally and abroad. Some of the most poignant moments of this time were not on our performance stages, but inside the small vans we rode in to get there. It was the circle that changed my mindset and transformed my heart. It was the people who surrounded me with whom I found redemption and hope for my heart.

I left Arizona a few years later, but the circle has endured up to my present. In fact, friends from that circle have stood by my side in some of the darkest times of my life. It's not been "the crowd" that supported me in the times of difficult transition. It hasn't been fans or followers who have come alongside when we received unwanted news or unexpected diagnosis. It's been that circle.

Over the last decade, I have had a keen awareness of the value of circles more than ever. When I became part of a business community, I thought I had plenty of friends and didn't need more. But over the course of my growth, I was more and more connected to an intimate group of other health coaches. This tight circle of leaders and business partners cultivated immeasurable growth in me.

In some ways, I'm the same Jen. Yet in other ways, I hardly recognize myself. My transformation didn't happen in a vacuum, nor did it happen up on the stage. It happened backstage, behind the scenes in coffee shops and living rooms and over internet calls with this community I now call my friends.

Life change happens in circles. When life hits the fan, when you need sound advice or just a friend to celebrate a win, you never head for a stage. Moments like these call for circles. These are the seasons when you reach out to friends from the circle. They see you. They know you. They have been part of the journey of your growth.

It's true that my platform and influence on and off stages has grown. But I did not do this alone. Yes, my personal journey toward health in the essential areas of my life—spiritual, emotional, physical and financial—began with a decision inside myself. But the road was not one I walked alone. As the African proverb says, "If you want to go fast, go alone. If you want to go far, go together."

I'm an independent woman. Fiercely independent. Some days that quality has saved my life. Other days, it's sabotaged me. As it relates to my journey of health and wellbeing, I did not do this alone. The decisions I've made as I have pursued health over the years have required moving away from the dysfunction of a life siloed in the areas where I needed the most help.

> *Having like-minded and like-hearted people around us is a powerful motivator.*

I have found health in a circle. I reached out to a health coach to create better habits that would be sustainable in any season of my life. I reached out to a business coach to help me create wealth that's led to a life of greater generosity and service. I reached out to a friend to pursue fitness accountability, and I reached out to a counselor to sort through some of my unwanted emotions. I reached out to a woman of faith to pursue an even deeper walk with Christ.

Having like-minded and like-hearted people around us is a powerful motivator. We are most influenced by the people we hang out with at home, work and play. Whether we are aware of it or not, our connections with people have a profound effect on our mood, our capacity, and our overall health.

In circles it can be easier to receive His word of increase over our lives. Increase for me and for you. Not necessarily an increase in followers—not always in ways measured by man. But increase in who God is.

I realize all this talk about finding your people and sitting in a circle can bring you back to a moment in time where you were uninvited or even cast out. I have those moments too. Nothing has pained me more than moments inside a circle. I've been uninvited to a gathering of old friends, begging the question, "Where do I fit? Who are my people?"

Being pushed out of a circle can put us in a position to strive for significance where we try to prove our worth. But let me remind you: the people who are meant to sit in your circle do not need you to do any of this. You have nothing to prove, only something to give.

A circle helped me see that. A small group of women helped me realize that. A table with other people in pursuit of Jesus and a desire to be content without settling enable that in me.

Who is in your circle? Do you need to find one or create one? Where is your common ground?

Perhaps it is time to take personal responsibility for the people you are surrounding yourself with or decide to stop going at it alone. If you want to create a healthy life, draw the right friends close and move away from the wrong ones. The right relationship is one that will help you on the journey, while the wrong one is one that actively sucks the life out of you.

You may first need to grieve the loss of old friends. I've had to. I've had to accept apologies I may never receive from people who wounded me in the past. Just don't allow yourself to remain handcuffed to what used to be. There's a new circle waiting for you—a new hope ready to break out. Take your next, brave step toward what is right for you: a circle of community, where you can know and be fully known.

CLOSING WORDS: CULTIVATING JOY

If you visit my Instagram account, you will see our family performing ridiculous dance moves to trendy, fifteen-second sound bites. One of the most common questions I am asked is, "How do you get your teenagers to dance with you on social media?"

The answer: throughout everything—the ups and downs, the doubts and fears, the transformation and breakthrough—I have learned the incomparable value of cultivating joy.

Family dance has been part of a healthy rhythm instilled in our home by intention. Dancing is one of the most powerful forms of human expression. It tells a story. It conveys emotions. It's a celebration, entertainment, healing, and worship. To dance is to connect.

It promotes confidence and self-esteem, encourages personal expression, and keeps our hearts beating.

The song selection has changed, and the music has been updated; but dancing has become part of our family culture. The day I have to force a kid to stand in front of the camera to make a social media video is the day I won't do it anymore. The goal for us is not to perform. The value is fun.

Dancing is a choice I have made in my home because I am committed to building a culture of joy. For me, for my family, for you.

Let's dig deeper into what God says about JOY and how we cultivate it.

I'll start with an unpopular opinion: I don't believe that joy is a choice. According to the Bible, it is actually a fruit of the Spirit.

"But the fruit of the Spirit is love, joy, peace, forbearance, kindness, goodness, faithfulness, gentleness and self-control."
Gal 5:22-23

You can cultivate joy in your life through the decisions you make. But primarily, it is a fruit grown by the Holy Spirit in your life. It is not something you can grow on your own. Joy is gladness, not based on your circumstances or your soul's desire to make it so. Joy is connected to your relationship with Jesus. It is the choice to have a connection with Him that produces joy in your life.

"Though you have not seen him, you love him; and even though you do not see him now, you believe in him and are filled with an inexpressible and glorious joy, for you are receiving the end result of your faith, the salvation of your souls." 1 Peter 1:8-9

In so many ways, this simplifies the process of cultivating joy. It is not determined by our ability to make a better choice. We can be released from the shame of not choosing joy, especially amidst struggles. Which is good because struggles are surprisingly vital to joy.

For many who know me, my life is often marked with joy. And that is true—but this joy has been born out of another word: grief. Heartache is part of my story.

I've never been able to stuff my emotions very well (we external processors tend to get things out into the open), so it surprised me to realize that I had been unconsciously avoiding feeling "sad" my entire life.

This epiphany happened in a therapy session with my husband. I listened as Marcus shared parts of his story causing him to feel sorrow. His therapist then turned to me and asked, "Jen, are you good with Marcus going through this process?" Immediately I responded, "Of course!"

The therapist then asked, "Why is that?"

"Because he's sad," I said. "So, let's solve it because who wants to be sad like this?"

Immediately a lightbulb went off. I had subconsciously set my goal to be "happy," but that was limiting and not very authentic. I realized it was time to be honest, and I began challenging myself to feel sadness, which is an integral part of life.

This work has taken me time. It's caused me to lay in bed with pajamas on at 2:00 PM, watching the latest Kardashians episode because I'm feeling sad (vs. my previous pattern of distracting myself with projects and Instagram). It's also enabled me to clear my calendar, disconnect my phone, and go to Disneyland with my family (something I would previously have labeled lazy, unwise, and unproductive). More significantly, sadness has invited me recently to embrace sorrowful mom moments as my oldest approaches her high school graduation.

Joy is magnified by the level of sorrow you allow yourself to feel.

How do you move forward with life-giving relationships when a friendship dies? How do you heal when a family member has broken your heart, the relationship is fractured, and you're uncertain if you will ever speak again? What happens when an unexpected diagnosis takes the breath out of your lungs, and you have no idea if the life you hoped for is even possible? What do you do when the mistake you made shifts the trajectory of your life, and you are scared about what that could mean? Or when the very thing you thought was the solution fails, and you need to start over again?

Grief is not quick or simple. It's deep. It's a loss. And it can take time. But getting honest with ourselves and God gives us the permission to feel. You cannot bypass grief to get to gratitude. That is where the JOY comes from.

> *I encourage you today to own your story. All of it.*

I encourage you today to own your story. All of it. The sadness in your life. The unwanted story, the unexpected situation, is fertile soil for joy. Because whether we like it or not, joy rises from the ashes of mourning.

Fortunately for us, sorrow is not the only thing the Holy Spirit uses to cultivate joy in our lives. According to the psalmist, praise feeds joy. In all circumstances and situations, we can bless the Lord, who guides us even if we don't fully understand His ways. We can praise Him with the knowledge that we will not be shaken. No matter what, He is right beside us. Tasting this truth is when our hearts fill with gratitude and assurance.

"No wonder my heart is glad, and I rejoice. My body rests in safety." Psalm 16:9 NLT

Joy also comes in the discomfort of being stretched yet still finding rest. When God wants to start something new, He always does it from a position of rest.

One summer, we took three weeks and traveled across the Atlantic to Italy and Greece. It was an incredible, exhilarating trip, filled to the brim with moments and memories I will never forget. When I arrived back home, someone asked me what I had learned on my trip. I liked this question because it enabled me to reflect on all the times God spoke to me. He spoke while I was enjoying gelato in Venice, sipping a cappuccino in Rome, and rolling pasta in Florence. He spoke when I was dipping warm pita in tzatziki in Crete. And He spoke while I was with friends sipping sweet, red wine in Santorini.

No matter where we are, there He is. He's God, and He is always with us. He has something to say to help us, even heal us. As I sat on a sofa back home, He confirmed what He said while I was sailing in the Mediterranean and staring out my back window at a water canal in Venice.

Rest doesn't have to come from vacation. We can get into a position of rest when we rely on God for His timing and results. Rest is a component of your joy quotient and the next step to fulfilling your destiny.

As I turn the pages of Scripture, it's clear to me that joy cannot be achieved through striving. Joy is an overflow of my connection to the Holy Spirit and is produced through my relationship with Jesus. Growing in joy means being closer to Him.

Being closer to Jesus doesn't happen by accident. It's a move I make—a step I take. I have learned this intention must be scheduled

"Joy is an overflow of my connection to the <u>Holy Spirit</u> and is produced through my relationship with Jesus."

on the calendar just like my other priorities. It requires incredible discipline and often some boundaries.

Jesus Himself was a prime example of someone who was committed to connection with the Father. In His humanity, He took on our limitations. He became human just like you and me. His body needed nourishment and rest. He felt our same pains and sorrows. And He operated in the same twenty-four-hour day we get every morning.

Jesus prioritized his own soul care *without feeling guilty*. He was the Son of God brought to Earth to save the people, yet He consistently separated Himself from people to spend time alone with God. Jesus lived in a rhythm of life that not only kept Him free from burnout but, far beyond that, it kept Him full of God. Walking in close communion with God brought joy.

Jesus was in tune with the Father, walking in closeness of relationship. He never sacrificed intimacy for any other agenda. As a result, He lived powerfully, compassionately and generously in response to needs, interruptions, and crises.

Unlike many of us, Jesus did not live on the defensive, overextending Himself, getting increasingly tired, and finally crashing. Instead, Jesus lived on the offensive. He proactively invested in His intimacy with the Father. And because He lived this way, He was never bulldozed by burnout.

These understandings about Jesus' way of life have helped me to command my calendar. It is not only *healthy*, but also *holy*, for me to schedule the time I need for journaling, reading the Bible, going to church, and worshiping through music in my own home. It's always good to have an organic, casual "conversation-prayer" throughout the day; but for me to live abundantly within my personal limitations, I need devoted time with Christ.

Part of commanding our calendar is understanding what our boundaries are. Personal boundaries are like property lines around our home—where our fence stands. What we value, what we're good at, and what we need and feel are inside our fence. Everything else is not.

Honoring ourselves through these boundaries is essential to all relationships and activities. The stronger our boundaries are, the greater our capacity to offer empathy and love to others. Good boundaries help us care for others because we have a stable foundation from which to operate and are not distracted or depleted by personal insecurities or blind spots.

This is why self-care and soul-care are important and not selfish. It's actually loving. Self-care is taking the measures and time to ensure emotional, mental, and physical wellbeing. Soul-care is tending to your spiritual health taking the measures necessary to keep your heart aligned with Christ.

It often starts with time spent with Jesus. Starting with Him enables us to keep saying "yes" when we feel like we're at the end of our rope, when grief overwhelms us, when discouragement and doubt subtly creep in. With Jesus as our priority, we can go another day. We have the courage to face another fight.

Jesus was a man under enormous pressure. Religious leaders wanted to kill him, the sick and broken constantly cried out for help, demons required banishing, and His preaching ministry took Him all over the countryside. But Jesus had no qualms about taking care of Himself. When He needed solitude, He took it. When He needed rest, He unapologetically rested, even sleeping on a boat in the middle of a storm. He even initially delayed when summoned to the bedside of His dying friend, Lazarus, which resulted in one of His most spectacular miracles.

He said no and yes when He needed to, yet He always succeeded in carrying out His mission perfectly. Why? Because He was utterly committed to the plans and purposes of God, no matter what. Like Jesus Himself, we too are filled with joy in the presence of God.

"I have loved you even as the Father has loved me. Remain in my love. When you obey my commandments, you remain in my love, just as I obey my Father's commandments and remain in his love. I have told you these things so that you will be filled with my joy. Yes, your joy will overflow!" John 15:9-11 NLT

I love the last part of this verse. "Yes, your joy will overflow." It's as if Jesus knows we need reassurance. He can hear our doubt after taking a step to submit. We begin to question when it doesn't work out after we have done our part. *Did God really say that? Is it for me? Is He even good?* This Scripture gives a resounding "yes." *Yes, joy is coming! Get ready.*

Just keep taking your next step. Just keep loving God and loving others. Everything may work out differently than you hoped, planned, or even expected. But that doesn't need to rob your joy. It's being brought to full completion exactly as God planned. So don't miss out on what He is doing. Just stay close to Him. *You can't miss it.*

Joy is guaranteed to abound when you stay in God's presence and trust Him to lead. Determine now to walk in closeness of relationship with Jesus. Refuse to sacrifice that intimacy for any other agenda. And as you do, you're invited into a life lived powerfully, compassionately and generously for Him. There's nothing else like it in all the world.

ABOUT THE AUTHOR

Jen Jones is passionate about personal transformation. Through her books, courses, conferences and groups, she equips and empowers women to create the life they love on a foundation of faith.

She is a certified health coach and has built a nationwide health and wellness business. She guides people on a path to help them take control of their health—mentally, physically and spiritually.

Jen and her husband Marcus are living a great adventure in San Diego, California with their four teenage children. Together they like to cultivate joy through dance videos, travel, family fun nights, and toes under the table.

Follow Jen on social media @jenjonesx4